Tales of an Island Innkeeper

TOLD BY
TONY LAPI

WRITTEN BY
BILL SCHREIBER

Copyright © 2025 by Tony Lapi

All rights reserved.

Published in the United States by Innkeeper Story LLC, Sanibel Island, FL

Trade Paperback Edition

ISBN-13: 979-8-218-55730-0

No portion of this book may be reproduced in any form without written permission from the publisher, except as permitted by U.S. copyright law.

Cover Illustration by Barry Braun

Cover Design by Cynthia McMillen

Author Photo by Nick Adams

Tales of an Island Innkeeper

Prologue

Out for a walk along a quiet stretch of beach, I paused a moment to consider the morning calm of the Gulf of Mexico, its lolling tide gently lapping the sugar-white sand. I spotted a few folks down the shoreline, toward the Sanibel Lighthouse, where they were bent over in the "Sanibel Stoop" as they searched for shells.

Closer by, a small flock of seagulls seemed to stand watch over a band of skittering sandpipers playing catch-me-if-you-can with the tide. The sight reminded me of watchful parents who have kept an eye on the children of families who have visited Sanibel and Captiva since the early days of the pioneers who settled these verdant strips of land, snugged like a crescent hug along the coast of Southwest Florida.

The moment's peaceful solitude coaxed a grin and converged with memories spanning fifty years living on these kindred slices of island paradise. The Gulf's sparkling surface, although serene in this moment, reminded me that, like life itself, the waters aren't always so calm. Nowhere is that more symbolically evident than in the Sanibel Lighthouse itself. Built in 1884, the landmark structure has withstood the test of time (and hurricanes over the past 140 years) to stand as a testament to the resilience of the islands and the determination of all who cherish them, whether longtime residents or visitors who return year after year.

In the ebb and flow of island life captured in these pages, I share tales from my experience spanning the five decades I have spent here as an innkeeper. Oh sure, my official title is chairman of the board of Sanibel Captiva Beach Resorts, but my life here didn't start that way.

No, life here started with a knot in my stomach and a feeling of, *What have I gotten myself into?* That was on an October day in 1976 when I stood on a crushed shell property along Captiva Drive and considered what would become today's 'Tween Waters Island Resort & Spa. Some fifty years ago, it sat as a ragtag gaggle of salty cottages their previous owners had destined for demolition. Gazing around the site, I tried to envision a top-notch resort destination as the no-see-ums began to feast on my ankles. (More on those dastardly little buggers later.)

Henry Ford, who seasonally called Fort Myers home back when he and Harvey Firestone were buddies with winter resident Thomas Edison, famously said, "Whether you think you can, or you think you can't, you're right."

I have to say the years have taught me that ol' Henry was right. My personal journey, and Sanibel Captiva Beach Resorts as it exists today, has been full of twists and turns. And despite my fancy title, at heart this innkeeper is just a kid who grew up along

Lake Ontario in Rochester, New York, and who enjoys helping people create memories to last a lifetime. It's all about the smiles.

Truth be told, I forged a life and helped build the business after being introduced to the winter warmth of Sanibel and Captiva five decades ago, just like those who still flock to our subtropical shores from colder climes. Like so many, I began my island flirtation as a snowbird and ended up falling in love.

Some folks call the personal and professional knowledge I've gained over my nearly eighty years of life "wisdom." While that may be true, I would add a few more descriptors: serendipitous, humbled, and grateful among them.

Of course, composing a life is about more than helping to build a company. Along the way, there have been lovably colorful characters, high-stakes personal and professional gambles, groundbreaking island events and traditions, mischievous shenanigans, musical capers, the challenges of battening down and battling back from hurricanes, fishy fish stories, and even some innkeeping insider intrigue. Yes, it's been quite a ride, and I've done my best to recall this passage of time the best I could.

As life has unfolded like the coming and going of the tides, it has been about people pulling together, in good times and tough times, to steward these special islands. All mixed with a sun-drenched dose of that same pioneering spirit that brought folks here in the first place and that makes Sanibel and Captiva such a wonderful place to live, work, visit, and play.

I hope you enjoy the ride through these pages as much as I have.

One

Upon These Shores

MAJESTIC BODIES OF WATER like the Gulf of Mexico have been a part of my life for as long as I can remember. Living and working on Sanibel and Captiva for some fifty years now, I spent my youth growing up a stone's throw from Lake Ontario, in Rochester, New York.

The Gulf and the easternmost Great Lake share some common characteristics—their sparkling grandeur attracts locals and visitors alike; sunsets beckon quiet reflection and a sense of awe, and their shorelines are great spots for a beach chair and a good book. Their average winter water temperatures, though? Yikes!

From January to April, peak tourist season on Sanibel and Captiva, the Gulf of Mexico lapping the islands averages about sixty-nine degrees, while Lake Ontario during those same months averages roughly thirty-seven degrees. Count me among those who would rather spend time on a sunny winter beach, where the only ice you have to worry about is in your beverage of choice.

Born in 1947, I was the youngest of five children in our close-knit Italian family. Two boys and three girls. We were first-generation Americans. My father arrived in the U.S. from Sicily when he was nine years old and grew up to become a physician; not bad for a kid who arrived from humble beginnings. I was lucky to live in a great neighborhood where everybody knew everybody else.

A public walkway to the lake ran by our house, so our family had the chance to visit folks as they headed for the water. Thanks to Lake Ontario, Rochester has one of the Great Lakes' best sand beaches. Then, as now, the lakeshore was a popular summer destination because of its boating, fishing, and swimming. Naturally, it drew plenty of visitors, and there were rental properties sprinkled around the neighborhood to accommodate them.

One such rental, next door to my family's house, attracted a constantly rotating band of bachelor buddies out for summer fun. Most of them were just starting their careers—some as lawyers and engineers, and others at the Rochester-based Eastman Kodak Company, whose innovative, pocket-sized "Instamatic" camera that launched in the early 1960s would allow millions of families to capture vacations, birthdays, weddings, and other special "Kodak moments" on film.

Little did I know as a skinned-knee kid rollicking around the neighborhood that helping to create such cherished memories would become a future focus of my life on Sanibel and Captiva.

As young teens, my older brother, Louie, and I got to know most of the next-door renters who came through. It was the early 1960s, and my parents were invited to their many parties. Curious about the renters' regular Saturday night bashes, Louie and I would slip over the next morning and have a few sips from the beer keg they hadn't quite managed to finish. Great way to start a Sunday, right?

We were just out exploring what life had to offer! Later that afternoon, my family would have a big Italian supper, and being in a chair around the table was mandatory, no matter what the other neighborhood rascals were up to. After supper, my brother and I would find our way outside to rejoin the neighborhood activities.

One of the regular renters next door was a guy named Lloyd Wright, who, decades later, would have a major role in the then-budding resort scene on these islands. Lloyd, a sandy-haired lawyer, was in his mid-thirties at the time and worked for a publishing company. It follows that he was very well read, very smart, and a great guy.

He knew a lot about a range of different subjects, not just the law. He had a strong entrepreneurial streak, traveled quite a bit, and enjoyed hosting neighborhood cocktail parties where everyone would get together to mingle and chat. He became good friends with my family—in fact, there was a time my brother and I needed assistance with our reading lessons, and he helped us improve our skills.

As it turned out, Lloyd enjoyed the rental house so much, he bought it and lived there year-round. Life unfurled from my small street in Rochester, through high school, and on into college, where I graduated from Syracuse University with a degree in bacteriology.

Given the path my life has taken, I would have never thought I'd ever put the scientific study of bacteria to use; boy, was I wrong. And, of course, college taught me critical thinking and how to analyze situations and solve problems. Those skills have served me well.

After college, I enlisted in the Army Reserve and worked as a part-time stevedore on the docks of Rochester, unloading massive ships carrying everything from mustard seed for French's mustard to canned tomatoes for Ragu spaghetti sauce.

The work could be grueling, particularly in the heart of a Lake Ontario winter, when temperatures can dip below zero and the wind can cut right through you. But I had always been used to hard work.

During this time, I built a boathouse at my parents' place and had to carve out a foundation hole in hard clay that was about twenty feet wide and fifteen feet deep. I ran a jackhammer six or seven hours a day and dug it out by hand. That was one of the house projects Lloyd took notice of over the years, recognizing my "can do" spirit and tenacity when presented with a task.

Twenty years my senior, Lloyd made note of my work ethic, which would play a key role in his decision to introduce me to Sanibel and Captiva's fledgling resort scene and mentor me in developing successful destination properties, thus opening the door to the opportunity of a lifetime.

But that momentous good fortune would forever take a back seat to another fortuitous event that would set the stage for the rest of my life: the serendipitous, circuitous, and improbable way I met the love of my life, Angie, my adventurous partner and wife of fifty-one years.

After college, I was back in Rochester, awaiting my duty post in the Army Reserve. My father had been afflicted with Parkinson's disease, and my parents were moving to a condo in Hollywood, Florida, located between Miami and Ft. Lauderdale. The move would allow my dad to escape the frigid winters, which would be beneficial for his health.

I drove their car down so they would have transportation as they began this new phase of their life, and I planned to fly back to Rochester after a week or so of helping them settle in.

On their trip to Florida, a kind United Airlines stewardess (as they were known back in the 1970s) named Angie Peluso assisted my father with his meal, and it made a lasting impression on both my parents. My genteel mother, touched by Angie's kindness, invited her to dinner, mentioning that their son (me) would also be there.

Angie was hesitant and offered Mom a polite smile as she gave the stewardess her condo phone number. Angie probably imagined a potential blind date disaster with some Quasimodo-like guy, and she threw the number away when she got home.

Back at the condo, my parents told me they'd met "a nice Italian girl," Angie Peluso, who might join us for dinner. There was a twinkle in my dad's eye when he told me she was a stewardess. Seemed my parents were eager to fix up their son and had chatted up an attractive sky-rider. What could go wrong?

A week passed, with no call from Angie, and I thought, okay, that was that. But fate had other plans. As I was boarding my return flight to Rochester, our paths crossed; serendipity's tap on the shoulder was in the form of her winged name tag: Miss Peluso. She wasn't originally scheduled to be on my route, but she had just happened to swap shifts with a co-worker. What were the odds?

I introduced myself and told her I was the guy my parents had mentioned as their son after she'd so kindly helped my dad on a flight the previous week. She seemed as surprised as I was, and she didn't immediately recoil from whatever Quasimodo image she might have had. So far, so good! Despite some initial awkwardness, we exchanged phone numbers and agreed to rendezvous during my next trip down to visit my parents.

Back in Rochester, I continued my temporary jobs while awaiting my Army orders. Meanwhile, Angie and I remained in sporadic contact. A month later, I returned to the Sunshine State, and we went out to dinner. We had a lovely evening and decided to keep in touch. My mother and father were thrilled, hoping their "nice Italian girl" and I would be a match.

However, she soon applied for a transfer to San Francisco as her home base instead of Miami, and I assumed she was out of the picture.

As months went by, I focused on helping my parents and thought my brief connection with Angie had ended. But I thought wrong. One day, by sheer luck (again!), Angie worked on a flight from Miami to Rochester, when the plot from a Hallmark Christmas romance movie unfolded.

After landing, she happened to meet the boyfriend of my father's secretary, Janice. A United Airlines agent in Rochester, he opened the airliner's door at the arrival gate, and there stood Angie. He recognized her name tag because I had told Janice—who was like a big sister to me—about this young lady named Angie Peluso, relaying that things were over before they really started because she was transferring to San Francisco and I'd probably never see her again.

However, with Dad's former office grapevine being alive and well, Janice had mentioned Angie to her boyfriend, the United Airlines gate agent. So he gave Angie a big spiel on what a great guy I was and encouraged her to call me. I was unaware of their chance encounter as the months continued to pass, still out of touch with her.

Fortunately, I was able to post with an Army Reserve unit in Florida, so I could look in on my parents on a regular basis. But at this point, I was certain Angie was out in California, our lives literally on opposite sides of the country and going in different directions. But fate smiled again. Her transfer fell through, and encouraged by the "he's a great guy" coaxing from Janice's boyfriend, Angie called me. It had been a good three or four months since we'd spoken, so for her to reconnect took me totally — and happily — by surprise.

With the bolt-from-the blue suddenness of that phone call, you could've knocked me over with a feather. We went out and had a really nice time, picking up where we had left off, and our relationship grew steadily from there.

Fast-forward to a beautiful marriage of fifty-one years, the two of us exploring the world together. Through all the near misses and chance meetings, Angie being on my parents' flight, and her simple act of kindness resulted in the most amazing blessing in my life.

Eventually, I finished my Army Reserve service, Angie and I got married, and we bought a home in Rochester. Still in my twenties, I needed to find work. Even as a kid, I had enjoyed working on house projects, so I started a small landscaping business. The work could be hard, but I didn't mind that; I had never been afraid to roll up my sleeves and get a job done.

Landscaping was the good news—the freshly cut grass, the neatly trimmed hedges, the blossoms in spring. But the bad news was a cold slap in the face: I had to switch to snowplowing in the winter.

Rochester averages about eight feet of snow a year, some driven by the brutally cold lake-effect snows coming off Lake Ontario. Still, I stuck with it, and Angie and I began to enjoy the start of our newlywed lives together.

The time back in the town of my birth allowed me to reconnect with Lloyd, and Angie and I began socializing with him and some of my classmates from college and high school. After a couple of years running the landscape/snowplow operation, I decided I would either have to grow the business or do something else. I tried teaching, but it wasn't for me.

What would I do with my life? How would Angie and I build a future? Serendipity had brought us together, but the road that stretched out before us—all 1,430 miles of it from Rochester to Sanibel and Captiva—would be one that required much more than luck.

Two

Toe in the Pool

During the time I served in the Army Reserve, helped cope with Dad's Parkinson's disease, and unknowingly weaved my way through a serendipitous maze that eventually led to Angie and I getting married, my longtime family friend Lloyd Wright from back in Rochester had started a new company called Rochester Realty.

Lloyd was a true entrepreneur and had a knack for recognizing opportunity. He had decided in 1973 to become a condominium developer on Sanibel. He began construction on Nutmeg Condominiums in 1974, and during construction the following year, he encouraged Angie and me to escape the Rochester winter and spend the winter of 1975-76 on Sanibel.

My landscaping/snowplow business had run its course up north, and Angie and I were trying to figure out a path forward in our lives, so we thought, hey, why not? Let's put our toe in the proverbial Sanibel pool. You never know where new experiences might lead. So, we headed south.

As I recount my arrival on the islands five decades ago, I must introduce a character that has been a constant companion: Mother Nature. She has blessed Sanibel and Captiva with stunning tropical beauty—lush fauna and foliage, unique marine life, pristine beaches, and glittering Gulf waters.

However, she can occasionally turn fierce in ways both calamitous and humbling. Hurricane Charley in 2004 was a stark reminder of that. The islands eventually rebounded from Charley's wrath. More recently, Hurricane Ian in 2022 was a disastrous blow, and 2024 Hurricanes Helene and Milton had us on edge.

As of this writing, the islands continue to build back stronger than ever, with a shared sense of resilience and community. All this is to say that my experiences beginning in the winter of 1975-76 are snapshots in time—and those images are nearly as plentiful as the shells that grace our beaches.

Driving across the Sanibel Causeway from the mainland's Punta Rassa for the first time, Angie and I soaked up the scene. The sparkling Gulf waters. Boats cutting frothy wakes on San Carlos Bay. Anglers fishing from the series of miniature sparkling-sand beaches that seemed as if an unseen hand had skipped stones to support the causeway where it swooped down to water level.

The verdant stretch of Sanibel Island drew near, its landmark lighthouse surveying the Gulf of Mexico's endless horizon as it had done since the late 1800s. As our wheels slowly *clip-clopped* over the causeway. We glanced at each other and exchanged hopeful grins—this coastal jewel had grabbed our attention.

As I drove onto the island and made a right turn onto Periwinkle Way, my thoughts were of the uncertainty in our lives. Was there a future for us here? How would we make it all work? We didn't have all the answers, but we knew we couldn't simply wait for the future to unfold in front of us. We had to make it happen.

During that winter season, I went to work for the Fort Myers general contractor Lloyd had hired to build his project. I reported to the head of Finger Construction Co., Ernie Finger, a longtime local presence in the construction industry. Ernie was as affable as he was skilled—his engineering mastery even allowed him to build and captain a sizeable concrete boat; there's something you don't see every day!

I was just a greenhorn in the hospitality business, and my first job wasn't a glamorous position by any stretch of the imagination. In fact, I got my hospitality feet wet—well, actually, I got my steel-toed concrete boots wet—pouring cement when I helped build the condo's community pool.

With its piping, pumps, filters, and finishes, it was a real education, and I learned how to operate it—knowledge that would prove extremely valuable down the road. Along with calloused hands, I developed an appreciation for the hard work frontline employees put in to make a destination property successful.

And I have to give Angie all the credit in the world for her ability to adapt to our new situation. We rented a tiny "hole in the wall" and set up our life amid the snakes, raccoons, opossums, and mosquitos behind the Sanibel Post Office located where Periwinkle Way intersects with Tarpon Bay Road.

The place was so tiny, I could make coffee without getting out of bed—only I couldn't make the coffee with the dwelling's well water, which smelled like rotten eggs. Luckily, within shouting distance was the iconic Bailey's General Store, which had served the island since 1899 and provided us with a convenient source of purified water for our java fix along with other groceries and supplies.

When Angie's father visited our cramped quarters, he spent most of his time in his camper; I guess he figured it was an upgrade! I'll never forget the Old World Italian *padre* looking around, taking in the joint where I had brought his daughter.

He shot me a sideways glance and said, "Seriously? Is this the best you can do?"

I knew he was really asking if we were nuts to move to a place that must have seemed like the end of the world to him. Still, while I worked with Lloyd on the Nutmeg project, Angie jumped in with both feet.

She set out to find a job and was hired by the fledgling City of Sanibel, which had just incorporated in 1974. There, she provided administrative support for the newly formed city and struck up a friendship with Porter Goss, who had been elected the island's first mayor. (Mayor Goss went on to carve out a remarkable career, including fifteen years in the U.S. Congress and a stint as director of the CIA.)

Angie made sure the crucial, publicly announced changes coming to the island's building regulations were never far from our minds as Nutmeg Condominiums rose.

One of those changes required developers to have more than fifty percent of their complex built by a certain date or their density allowance (the number of permissible units) and setback (an area where no structures could be built) could be adversely affected.

That set off alarm bells. If Lloyd didn't accelerate the project, he would be in jeopardy of losing six prime Gulf-front units, which would mean economic disaster. Kicking it into a higher gear with Finger Construction, we worked our tails off and met the requirement in the nick of time.

Fronting the Gulf, Nutmeg Condominiums became a hotspot for both year-round living and vacation getaways. The price for the two-bedroom, two-bath floor plans hit $100,000, which set a record for Sanibel at the time. Known as Nutmeg Village today, it's not unusual for units to sell for well over $1-million. I guess you could say Lloyd's entrepreneurial vision is still alive and well on West Gulf Drive.

All this unfolded in the face of a condominium market that was in dire straits in the mid-1970s, which turned out to be a bad news/good news situation. The bad news was that the Nutmeg units weren't selling at the pace Lloyd had expected. This amped up his uneasiness about his long-range plans. Maybe he should pivot from being a developer who built and sold properties to a hotelier, who bought and operated long-term instead. The idea of being an innkeeper was suddenly in the salty air.

Fortunately, along with the bad news about the condominium market came some good news: the current owners of 'Tween Waters Inn—Scott Hamilton and Jay Friedberg of Louisville, Kentucky—had planned to build condominiums at the 'Tween

Waters site, but the market downturn caused them to abandon that idea and put the property up for sale.

Having witnessed firsthand the industriousness I had demonstrated dating back to my boyhood in the old Rochester neighborhood, Lloyd recognized that hard work was in my DNA and asked me if I might like to be an innkeeper and build a premier destination property from the ground up.

Wait, what? An innkeeper? Was he crazy? What kind of future was in that? At the time, you could shoot a cannon on Captiva and practically nobody would hear it. I mean, talk about being in the middle of nowhere! And the property sat on such a narrow stretch of the island you could drive a golf ball the roughly 300 yards from the bay side to the Gulf.

The day came when Stan Johnson, the then-owner of Priscilla Murphy Realty—which in the early 1950s became one of Sanibel's first realty office locations—took Lloyd on a strolling look around 'Tween Waters' forty-seven cottage units.

Lloyd's reaction? "Get me out of this dump." (If he had ever seen where Angie and I were living at the time, he would've thought the vintage 'Tween Waters in its weatherworn shape was Shangri La!)

As I talked with Angie about the idea of possibly becoming the innkeeper at 'Tween Waters, I couldn't help but recall the day a year ago when we had first motored across the causeway. My new companion, Mother Nature, had provided a visual clue about the promise and potential peril of a turn into the unknown: along with the staggering beauty that had greeted us, there had also been a stretch of deeply bruised sky as a storm rumbled out on the Gulf.

I told Lloyd I wasn't sure. He understood my hesitancy. It would be a major life commitment with no guarantees.

When the day came that it was time to either go big or go home, Lloyd suggested, "Why don't we take a second look? Let's do our due diligence, gather all the information we can about the prospects, and then make the decision."

As crunch time loomed, I was in my late twenties, and I'm clear-eyed about the fact that I was a mere worker bee and Lloyd was the visionary. So, in the summer of 1976, I accompanied him on several exploratory trips to visit the property to learn everything we could. We needed to see all the angles.

One of those crucial angles was that the owners had already secured valuable water permits for their planned conversion to condominiums. This was critical because there was a moratorium on such permits, which would have made it impossible for us to expand 'Tween Waters. We knew that if we purchased the property, we couldn't economically sustain it with just the existing forty-seven cottage units and an outdated restaurant.

The necessary permits that transferred with the purchase became a major factor in our decision. So, on October 18, 1976, we rebranded the original Rochester Realty as Rochester Resorts and bought 'Tween Waters for $1.2 million. And life was about to get much more complicated as I found my way through a lifetime's worth of days, both sunny and stormy.

Three

Winds of Change

As I surveyed the newly purchased 'Tween Waters site with Lloyd, I did my best to put on a brave face. Before us sat forty-seven sunbaked cottages in various stages of disrepair that would require significant work if we hoped to provide the quality guest experience we envisioned.

Meanwhile, my only experience in the resort hospitality business had been in concrete-caked boots as a twenty-eight-year-old junior laborer working through sunburn and sweat-stung eyes on the community pool and the building at Nutmeg Condominiums, where Angie and I would soon live for ten years.

Now, only months after sloshing around in wet cement, Lloyd had taken me under his wing in this ambitious endeavor to polish this decaying diamond in the rough, trusting I could play a major role in managing its transformation into a successful business. The pressure was on.

I was entering a new world. What did I know about the intricacies of real estate development or commercial renovation and construction management? Or working with architects? Or permitting? Or recruiting and supervising a resort staff? I was coming off a residential landscaping and snowplow business!

Fortunately, when it came to leadership, I would need to rely on a formative experience from decades ago and dust off skills I had developed way back in military prep school, where I had been a company commander my senior year and was responsible for overseeing ninety others.

On top of guest facilities and services, staff team-building, and the operational aspects of the business, I would have to figure out the restaurant side of things, a tricky business even in the best of times. This included recruiting, training, and maintaining a talented culinary staff, along with developing a menu that would fit with what we wanted to do.

Was I excited? Jittery? Apprehensive about the day-to-day challenges and obstacles? Yes! All of that! I felt like I had just jumped into a ten-foot-deep pool with a five-foot air hose and could only hope my willingness to work hard and paddle even harder would allow me to keep my head above water.

Even though the sunny temperature hovered in the mid-seventies and there was a refreshing onshore Gulf breeze whispering through the palms, I broke out in a cold sweat on our first day as partners walking the site. We stopped to consider one of the ramshackle cottages on the bay side. The only thing racing faster than my heart was my mind, grasping for answers to how the heck I was going to find my way through all the unknowns that lay ahead.

"Well, Tony, what do you think?" Lloyd's voice jammed the brakes on the locomotive of thoughts thundering in my mind.

Squinting behind my sunglasses at the unit's peeling paint, I reached out with a finger and flicked off a brittle flake, and I knew there was only one way forward. "I think we better start swimming like hell."

He nodded. "I know you've never been afraid of a little hard work." I gave him a sideways glance and spied a slight grin creasing his face.

"A little hard work?!" my inside voice yelled. I knew this endeavor would be a heavy lift, exponentially beyond anything I had been involved with in my entire life. But Lloyd seemed willing to bet my work ethic and the determination I had demonstrated since I was a kid would be enough. He was nearly fifty at the time and had seen and done a lot in his life. I was approaching thirty and ready to see where life would take me. Lloyd was someone I looked up to, and he saw potential in me. I was intrigued by that.

At that moment, with the breeze rustling my hair and my imagination, the confidence he had placed in me since I was a youngster rolled in like a wave, and I decided I would ride that wave to whatever distant shore awaited.

That decision in 1976 quickly led to the equally pivotal years of the late 1970s and early 1980s, as change blew in faster than a summer squall. 'Tween Waters at this time was in rough shape. It's difficult to maintain a property in a harsh saltwater environment, and the past had not only taken its toll on the deteriorating original cottages but had also put their future in precarious jeopardy.

During the approximately five-year period from 1978 to 1982, you might say we were getting our sea legs as our dream of building a premiere beach destination turned into solid structures, and our aspirations began to take tangible shape. These were the years we laid the foundation, not just in concrete, but in the relationships and community building that would define our properties for decades to come.

Mother Nature reminded us right off the bat that she would be a constant force to contend with, even if that force was pint-sized. An early nemesis in our inaugural efforts to salvage our opportunity was the party crashers known locally as no-see-ums, virtually invisible little hellions that love to feast on whatever skin they can latch on to.

And here's a tidbit for your next game of Florida Trivial Pursuit: they're in the class of biting midges, and there are more than 4,000 species, with forty-seven of those calling the Sunshine State home. They literally hid out beneath our feet, under the wooden deck slats around the pool we were building, our legs serving as their snack bars. Of course, we had to nickname this early resort gathering spot the poolside No-See-Um Bar.

But in true *Little Engine That Could* fashion, we were determined to follow our dream by constructing brand-new units. The first ten we built were on the bay side, which the contractor turned over to us in late December 1977.

We had just a handful of days to furnish the one-bedroom suites, an endeavor that felt like a frantic race against time if we were going to capitalize on any of the remaining tourist season that winter. There were no elevators. Just a band of us huffing and groaning and sweating as we hauled furniture up the stairs, piece by piece.

In 1978, the bike path through J.N. "Ding" Darling National Wildlife Refuge was approved, the Southwest Florida International Airport officially opened, and the Bee Gees had dance floors discoing the night away with top Billboard hits "Stayin' Alive" and "Night Fever."

It was also a year when we produced some big hits of our own, completing both the Palmetto building on the bay side and the Sea Grape building on the Gulf side, each with thirty-two rooms. Combined with the ten guest suites in the Gumbo Limbo building, that gave us seventy-four new rooms to fill.

Our "office," a modest trailer that had a slight tilt to it, was a creaky nerve center of operations beginning in 1977 until the end of 1978. We began with no telephones or other modern amenities.

Of course, this was way before cell phones and the internet. This was back in the "carbon copy" days. (Kids, ask your parents, or maybe even your grandparents, what carbon paper was! While you're at it, ask them what a fax machine was—which we also didn't have in the late 1970s!) We made do with a lot of grit and teamwork.

Fun Fax Fact: I believe 'Tween Waters had the first fax machine ever on Sanibel and Captiva—yes, even before the real estate offices! This came about because one of our long-term guests, a corporate executive from a tech-savvy major city who had been using the newfangled communication machines, told me that if we had a fax available for visitors to use, they could stay longer because they could continue to do business while they stayed with us.

So sometime around 1980 we poured around $2,000 into a fax machine, an astronomical price at the time, and equivalent to roughly $6,500 today. Still, that whirring machine with the coated rolls of paper paid for itself many times over, helping to extend people's stays. Its *beep-boop-beep* followed by a series of screeches indicating its communication with another far-off fax was music to my ears and a much welcomed new revenue stream for our budding resort.

As our grand opening approached, it was like the feeling you get when you're in a roller-coaster car and its *click-clacking* beneath you as it methodically ascends the rails to the highest point on the tracks before sending you on a thrill ride—for us, that was March of 1978, the peak of the tourist season.

There would be no warm-up in the slower off-season months. We could all feel the approach of our unveiling, and sensed things were about to get wild. I mean, we had seventy-four brand-new rooms to fill, all while working out of a tipsy trailer with a makeshift reservation system—and I use the word "system" loosely.

Everything was done by hand with a staff that was still learning. And that's when things got truly exciting, in a flying-by-the-seat-of-our-pants kind of way. Someone would pop into the trailer. "Hey, how are ya?" went the typical greeting. "You have any rooms?"

"Welcome to 'Tween Waters! You bet we have rooms!" our smiling desk attendant would reply. "Just fill out this registration form and get ready to hit the beach!" In about sixty seconds, guests would head for the door, ready for their island escape.

"No, no, no, wait!" the attendant would smile and call after them. "You don't want to forget these." And we'd hand the guests their room drapes and bedspreads.

We were literally just winging it as we went along. And by and large, those early guests seemed to enjoy being part of a shared adventure. It was chaotic, but it was also exhilarating. I often thought of us as assembling a ship as we sailed it.

The poolside No-See-Um Bar quickly became a guest hotspot, which founding staffer Timmy Jardas operated six days a week. He was a fair-skinned guy with reddish hair and had a tendency to talk at a fast clip. I think it was because his mind processed information so rapidly; he had an amazing knack for figuring out how things worked and was a quick learner.

I had known Timmy, a gifted jack-of-all-trades kind of guy, from way back in Rochester. Ten years my junior, he actually took over my boyhood paper route when I moved on from delivering newspapers. Years later, when I started the landscaping business, I asked him to come to work for me mowing lawns.

He shifted on his feet for a brief moment before answering. "Tony," he said, "I've known you a long time, but you have to understand that if you hire me, I have a handicap."

"A handicap? What are you talking about?"

"Well, one of my legs is shorter than the other."

I thought about that for a second before responding, "Well, shoot, that's perfect. You can mow the sides of the hills." We both busted up laughing, and from then on I knew we would make a good team.

The No-See-Um bar certainly lived up to its name, as the pesky nibblers would flit around at dusk and leave our guests with polka-dot legs. Fortunately, not even the uninvited party crashers could quash the vacation spirit. The pool bar became a big hit and the social heart of the resort.

In March, our busiest time of the year, a room would go for around $42 a night—a price that seems unimaginable now. But back then, it was enough to keep us afloat and drive our growth.

By the end of 1978, we had built a new office, moving out of the trailer and into a more permanent structure. Initially, we hadn't planned to build an upper floor on the office, but we ended up designing a two-bedroom unit above it.

Lloyd and I each had a small office in the first-floor space, navigating the challenges of setting up a switchboard and running phone lines to all the cottages. Slowly but surely, we were moving from a by-the-seat-of-our-pants setup to a more organized operation.

Still, not everything was smooth sailing. The day would come when we hit 100 units and were able to acquire a liquor license before we built the Crow's Nest in 1981. We had this little bar in the original kitchen, which was not air-conditioned at the time. The summer temperatures could get sultry in there, so all the booze would get pretty warm.

During one of our all-hands-on-deck periods, Lloyd was a bartender for a while, and he had to get drinks out to our guests before all the ice melted in the glasses and the drinks got watered down, but he got pretty good at moving quickly so the beverages remained refreshing and enjoyable.

Thinking back on these startup years, I realize Lloyd really took a big chance putting me in charge. But honestly, I wanted to prove myself. And after a while, I started to feel like I belonged in my role. Yes, he handed me the ball as the quarterback, and I had to move the team down the field.

I found ways to get things done, even though new and challenging issues kept coming my way. I had to learn to adapt, keep working through a to-do list that constantly grew, and tackle the unexpected challenges that popped up.

I didn't want to disappoint Lloyd, myself, or Angie, who was a real rock for me during that time. She went out and got her real estate license and started earning money, which was a huge help. She always said they weren't paying me enough for the amount of work I was doing. And she was probably right, because I was working ungodly hours while wearing about a dozen different hats and tackling a gamut of challenges to keep things going. But luckily, she had a job as well, and it gave us some security while I kept pursuing this opportunity to do what I loved. I'm blessed she put up with it.

The opportunity Lloyd introduced became a delicate balance of mutual respect. I had known him since back in the old Rochester neighborhood, when I was a teen and he was in his mid-thirties. Twenty years on, there was this natural dynamic of him as a mentor. On the one hand, I appreciated the experience he had.

But on the other, it was sometimes a challenge to find a balance between respecting his position and asserting my own voice. Sometimes that meant pushing back. We were both strong personalities. We had our differences over the years, and things got heated now and then. I mean, I come from a Sicilian background, so I can have a bit of a temper. And Lloyd? Well, after all those years, let's just say he knew how to push my buttons.

One day, we were crammed into our tiny office space when an argument escalated, and before I knew it, I'd lost my cool. In a fit of frustration, I put my fist through the door of his office, which was next to mine. Of course, I knew it was a hollow-core door, so I wasn't worried about breaking my hand, but it sure made an impression—I think both of us were a bit taken aback.

Lloyd stared at the gaping hole in his door for a few stunned seconds. "Well, that's just great, Tony. Now hand over your door to replace it."

Without missing a beat, I turned around and punched a hole through my own door. "There," I shot back. "Now they match."

The next day, we were both over it. Remember, we had a long history, and we'd developed a natural pull-and-tug, you might say, as I had grown into a young man pressing my independence. This give-and-take was just a part of our relationship, and I've always believed that if you get mad, you've got to get over it quickly. You can't carry that stuff with you for long.

When all was said and done, Lloyd and I didn't allow the tensions that would flare up from time to time to get in our way of continuing to develop 'Tween Waters.

Not all the improvements during this time were necessarily readily visible; in addition to the new units, we also undertook major infrastructure improvements. One of those was building our own on-site water treatment plant and getting the Sea Grape units connected to it; soon after, we would also connect all the other units, cottages, and the restaurants.

The water treatment facility, which we still operate, was a crucial improvement over the septic tanks relied upon by the earliest units we inherited—not only for our growth and functionality, but also for protecting the island's beautiful environment. We understood how delicate our coastal habitat was, so upgrading from the old septic tanks allowed us to play our part in protecting what makes Captiva so special.

Constructing the plant led to my first experience renting and operating a tractor with a backhoe on it to help drive the sewer-system transition. Getting the cottages and restaurants hooked into the system was a grueling task, but with the help of a plumber named Remo, we managed to get it done.

Running that rental tractor and backhoe became second nature to me—so much so that we eventually bought our own rig. That decision was driven by necessity and a bit of ingenuity.

Soon after we had purchased 'Tween Waters and managed to get the existing restaurant up and running, we discovered that the facility's electrical service was not only inadequate, but dangerous. So we spent a lot of time rewiring it and putting in a new 800-amp service, which was a really big investment for us.

We had a generator set up to kick in when we lost power. The problem was, it wasn't *enough* power, and we didn't have the money for a large commercial generator. So I did some research. What I learned was that if I bought a tractor, which we could use in multiple traditional ways, I could use the machine's drive shaft to hook up and run added emergency power through a smaller generator without compromising too much. I mean, we couldn't run the air-conditioning system, but we could supplement power to the crucial food refrigeration banks and the kitchen's exhaust fans.

Here again, I was feeling my way along in the innkeeping business. We needed a cost-effective solution to a problem, and I was able to figure a way forward to a great degree with a little outside-the-box thinking. We had the resources to finance a tractor and have a serviceable generator powered by its drive shaft. I figured this approach, unlike trying to buy a huge commercial generator, wouldn't cost us an arm and a leg, when just keeping the doors open took all the appendages we had.

An innkeeper's work is never done! I laid the concrete block for the platform to support what would soon be our dedicated emergency generator to replace the makeshift one I had rigged using the drive shaft of our tractor.

Our operations truly had an amazing start during this five-year stretch. I was hopeful about the future and I could feel our confidence growing. Leave it to Mother Nature, that constant companion we all live with, to remind me who's in charge. It was a harrowing experience with my tractor on the day I had to activate its power-generating capability during a raging thunderstorm that had knocked out our power. Rain blew sideways, stinging my face like little pins, and jagged webs of lightning ripped across the charcoal-colored sky. And here I was, in the maelstrom, wiring the tractor to run the generator and save our food. Luckily, Ben Franklin, who invented the lightning rod to protect buildings from lightning damage, would be happy to know I didn't turn into one of those rods during that storm!

Recalling the monumental undertaking to build this system makes me chuckle and shake my head, because I realize my degree in bacteriology from Syracuse, which I had thought would never come in handy, actually did! It allowed me to understand some of the issues surrounding the plant's operations. Eventually, rooted in that scientific discipline, I was able to learn even more.

Today, we continue to maintain the entire system in-house, and during our busiest season, we'll treat about 30,000 gallons a day. Who would have thought that a sewer plant project could be a pretty amazing experience?

From working to revitalize the original cottages, to building seventy-four all new accommodations, to acquiring additional vacation properties on the islands, the years 1978 to 1982 were a period when we transformed from a scrappy startup into a fledgling company. We learned as we went, often through trial and error, but always with an eye on the future as we overcame challenges and created the foundation of our success.

That expanding foundation, however, gave rise to some growing pains, particularly when it came to staffing. Finding, training, and keeping a growing staff happy can be a challenge, but one that must be met to maintain top-quality service across multiple locations, all while maintaining the irresistible charm we were working so hard to establish.

Four

The Heartbeat of Hospitality

It's been said that the longest journey begins with the first step. For 'Tween Waters, it began with the many, many steps of those who played a part in what has unfolded over these past fifty years. Those steps belong to the people who have made it all happen: the employees who put in long, hard hours to help grow 'Tween Waters from its humble beginnings into the amazing vacation oasis it is today.

Our expansion with the Sea Grape building and the Palmetto building was just the beginning. Our horizons expanded even further in 1979, when we acquired the Beachview Cottages. On top of that, in 1982, we added Castaways Beach & Bay Cottages. This rapid-fire growth would dramatically impact our staffing needs.

It can be tricky when you're trying to recall everyone who has crossed your path going back a half-century, but there were plenty of colorful island characters, each contributing to the resort's growth and unique charm. Many of these employees stayed with us for years, helping to shape the resort's identity, and some are still with us decades later. They became more than just staff; they became part of our resort family.

With longtime former employees from the early years. Front row (left to right): Keith, Jeff, Yours Truly, Carole, Don. Middle row: Renee, John, Janie, Tara, Kathy, Kitty. Back row: Timmy, Heather.

One unforgettable personality was a woman everyone knew as "Tall Beth." She ran the office and knew the locals—crucial when you're the new kid on the block on a tiny, remote island. She dated a well-known fishing guide, the renowned Bob Sabatino.

Bobby was a real fixture around here. He came down from New York in the 1950s, long before the Sanibel Causeway was built in 1963, and became one of the best guides these islands have ever seen. Islanders still remember him fondly, and for good reason. He had a way with the water, and a following that stretched far beyond our little corner of the world.

Unlike most of the crew, Tall Beth didn't live in the dilapidated "barracks" located behind the sun-beaten restaurant. She lived in unit 110, a small courtyard unit. Our one and only housekeeper for forty-seven units, John, was a dead ringer for being a member of rocker Alice Cooper's band. There was no maintenance crew to speak of, but then again, things were in such bad shape, we had trouble fixing anything anyway.

Tom Hicks ran the marina back then—a dependable guy, always had a smile, even when the work was tough. Then there was Barefoot Tom. Now, that guy was something else. A big, burly fellow, he had this uncanny ability to walk on sandspurs and shards of broken shells without flinching. It was like his feet were made of leather. His room in the employee barracks was a sight to behold—suffice to say, it was as rough around the edges as his heels were.

And then there was Ruth Crist. She was the bookkeeper when I first arrived, but I had to let her go because I didn't need a bookkeeper—not that she wasn't good at her job, but we didn't have much in the way of money to keep track of.

Funny enough, Ruth stuck around and lived below the marina office on a dirt floor, with her saltwater aquarium and her beloved dog, Fiddler. She was a bit quirky, to say the least, but she had a good heart. I was able to hire her back later on to help with the bank deposits when our finances improved.

As we grew and expanded, we hired more employees for the restaurant, housekeeping, and front desk. One standout was Holly Monroe, a redheaded gal from Bolton Landing, New York. Her mother had worked cleaning houses on Captiva, and Holly followed in her footsteps.

Little did I know that Holly would steadily perform in a manner that would see her work her way up to become our controller and a steadfast part of our team for the past forty-four years and counting. Pretty amazing.

Another one of our early shining stars was a waitress, "Mama" Betty Richardson. In her mid-fifties or so, she had a delightful North Carolina accent and took tremendous pride in her work. Each day she'd arrive in her neatly pressed uniform, looking like she'd just been to the hairdresser. She was the epitome of a great waitress. Attentive, personable, and conscientious.

"Mama" Betty (second from right) shares a laugh with Margaret (left), Millie and Timmy during one of our Oktoberfest celebrations.

She was also a colorful character who would get into verbal spats back and forth with our chef during some of our super busy serving times. His name was Tony, and because we shared first names, he was known as Chef Tony, while I was nicknamed Boss Tony.

Mostly, Mama Betty and Chef Tony's bickering was a lot

of good-natured call-and-respond squabbles, and she would sometimes make hilarious off-the-cuff remarks that kept us all in stitches, adding a much-appreciated dash of humor during otherwise stressful meal times.

In those days, when we hit the slow, off-season periods, we had what we called the "bleed" shift, so named because its initials were BLD, which stood for breakfast, lunch, and dinner. Sometimes that entire shift consisted of one person who covered all three meals. This occurred on one particularly crazy morning while we served breakfast. Mama Betty was hustling around the kitchen and she slipped, ending up in a rather painful-looking split.

I rushed over, worried she was seriously hurt. "Are you okay, Betty?" I asked, my voice laced with urgency as other kitchen staff hurried to her aid.

She looked up at me and quipped, "I think I might have split my private lady parts!"

It was unexpected, and it cracked us all up, especially since she usually carried herself in such a ladylike manner. She picked herself up and went about her business, keeping the food operation running smoothly. Unvarnished moments like these kept the camaraderie strong and reminded us to find humor even in the busiest times.

This was incredibly important because, from the outset, I've learned that this business is not just about providing a place to stay; it's about building relationships and creating a staff community that feels like family.

One of the first names that comes to mind when I reflect on those days in housekeeping is Maggie White. Maggie was a true character, and you couldn't help but like her. Seven days a week, she worked tirelessly in housekeeping during the day and then served in the dining room at night, waiting on such prominent figures as J.N. "Ding" Darling, after whom the national wildlife refuge on Sanibel is named.

A powerhouse, Maggie and her partner would arrive from up north year after year to work the winter tourist season, an arrangement that was much more common back then than it is today.

As a steward of an expanding portfolio of properties, the company's need for more and more housekeeping staff led to some memorable experiences. Because we couldn't find all the help we needed on the islands, we bought a van to transport staff from Fort Myers.

At the end of each workday, they would take the van home, keep it overnight, and return the next morning. The honest truth is, these were women of various ages who came from challenging neighborhoods that were the legacy of racial segregation and harmful Jim Crow-era laws, which opened my eyes and inspired me with their spirit of resilience and determination.

One of the standouts was named Ethel, a large woman with an equally large personality. She seemed to fill the matronly shoes among the younger housekeepers, and she was in charge of driving the van. She did a fantastic job, ensuring things ran smoothly—albeit with an unconventional method during one indelible episode.

I'll never forget the day I opened the van door to find pin-drop silence and wide-eyed stares. Normally, there was lively chatter among the group. I wondered what the heck was going on, so

I pulled Ethel aside and asked her what had happened to make everyone so quiet. She explained with a candidness I came to appreciate.

"Well, I'll tell you, the girls were really rowdy, and I told them over and over to pipe down so I could concentrate on driving. The thing was, they wouldn't listen."

Figuring she had to get their attention another way, she had pulled out her gun! She didn't hear another peep after that, she told me with a slight grin.

After I picked my jaw up off the crushed shell parking lot, I gave her a friendly pat on the shoulder. "Jeez, Ethel, I understand your frustration, but we can't have you packing a gun, for heaven's sake." It was too dangerous for all concerned, including her! Of course, she understood, and we carried on our cordial relationship for many years to come.

Ethel's unique way of speaking also left an impression on me. She told me about her husband, a "swimper," and she would often ask me if I wanted any "swimps," which I eventually came to understand were shrimp. I also learned her husband's shrimp were delicious! It's tough to beat fresh shrimp right off the boat.

I valued my relationship with Ethel and I always think fondly of her. She helped me understand and appreciate the differences in our life experiences, as our interactions highlighted the cultural richness within our expanding team, providing me opportunities for personal growth.

Listening to and valuing employees was something I prioritized. On one occasion I'll never forget, practicing this approach led to a disturbing discovery. As our housekeeping staff grew,

I would check in with them to get their feedback and see how everything was going.

One day, I stopped in, and they mentioned they weren't receiving the tips from guests they used to. This was a big deal, especially during the peak tourist season, when tips were an essential part of their income.

What the heck was happening? I had to find out. To begin, I decided to start at the top, with our housekeeping supervisor, Ted. I asked the front desk staff about Ted's daily arrival times.

"Does he usually ask for a list of rooms where the guests have checked out?" I inquired.

The desk staff confirmed that he often arrived before the housekeeping staff, and yes, he got the report on rooms that had been vacated.

The next morning, I arrived earlier than usual, before Ted had a chance to show up. I selected a room where guests had recently checked out and placed a mock Thank You note along with some paper cash, of which I had made copies.

I then watched from a concealed spot as Ted entered the unit and exited shortly thereafter. Once he was gone, I checked the room; the note and the money were missing. This alone wasn't completely incriminating; if he had stripped the room of linens, he could have picked up the note and the cash and given them to the room's deserving housekeeper. But he hadn't.

I called him into my office. "Ted," I began, "you don't have to be the sharpest tool in the shed to work for me, but your integrity has to be impeccable. Today, I'm here to question your integrity."

I laid out the evidence: what I had observed of him going into the room and the copies of the bills he'd taken. He was flustered and tried to justify his actions by claiming the housekeepers owed him money. "Whoa, whoa, whoa," I interrupted. "That doesn't cut it. You can either resign right now or I'll inform the housekeepers of your actions and we'll see what they would like to do."

Ted resigned on the spot. I immediately went to the housekeepers and explained that Ted no longer worked with us, apologizing for his actions. I assured them that we would keep a tighter watch on their tips and their working environment.

Not only had he been robbing them of the money, but he had also been robbing them of the personal satisfaction each housekeeper would have had from a grateful "thank you" for a job well done. This episode reinforced my commitment to the staff to ensure they felt valued and respected.

This incident was a significant learning moment, and it has always stayed with me. It all boils down to integrity and taking responsibility to ensure your supervisors are doing what they say they're doing and not getting too carried away with their own sense of power or testing what they can get away with.

Equally important, I learned how crucial it is to listen to your frontline employees, especially if they're having issues with a supervisor. When you start hearing the same concerns from different folks, it's a sign that there could be a problem that needs addressing. It all comes down to character. That's the thing you always want to keep an eye on. It's the foundation of everything, and it's what makes all the difference in the long run.

Fortunately, incidents such as that were rare. Overall, our entire staff built a sense of community and camaraderie. A great example was our annual staff Christmas parties, when the housekeeping staff and the guys who worked at the marina would come together. The women would arrive dressed to the nines, looking like they were attending a New Year's Eve ball. It was so wonderful, a time when toasts were lifted to celebrate our accomplishments that year and everyone would dance the night away. It was a joy to see the housekeeping staff having such a good time.

On a more somber note, one of my most poignant memories from those days was the loss of a housekeeper to AIDS. This was before the disease was widely understood. She had a radiant smile, often showcasing some gold teeth—which I came to understand is considered a symbol of independence, pride, and resilience in the African-American community.

I attended her funeral, held in a sweltering church in Fort Myers, and it was a powerful celebration of life. The singing and uplifting spirituality left a profound impact on me, underscoring the strength and bond of their community.

Housekeeping has always been the heart and soul of the hospitality business. Providing a clean and welcoming environment is crucial for guest satisfaction. My experiences with the early housekeepers, particularly the team of African-American women I supervised in the 1970s, taught me the importance of mutual respect and integrity in building a successful business.

These women faced socioeconomic challenges that were starkly different from my own experiences. Working to understand their backgrounds and the obstacles they often faced deepened my appreciation for their hard work and determination.

Sometimes, I'll spot a guest I've known through the years out on the beach at sunset, and I'll go out to say hello. After our chat, I'll stand there looking out over the Gulf of Mexico, just soaking it all in. There's a calm on the water, the waves kissing the beach.

When I turn around to head back to 'Tween Waters, I'll sometimes scratch my head and wonder, how did I accomplish all this? And I'll realize that it wasn't just me. Lloyd certainly lit the flame, and then I worked like crazy to fan that flame, along with having the good fortune to have worked with tremendous people from top to bottom.

I'm eternally grateful to all those who played a role and helped launch 'Tween Waters on a trajectory that continues to this day. We built more than just a resort; we built a community, a place where employees became family.

The contributions of those early staff members, with their diverse backgrounds and unique personalities, were invaluable. To this day, I carry with me the memories and the lessons they taught me during those formative years, years that set the stage for the incredible journey that was yet to come.

Five

Guests Become Friends

THE YEARS SPANNING 1978 to 1982 were filled with challenges, but they were also blessed with encounters with remarkable people who left an enduring impression on the history of our little slice of paradise. Over the past fifty years on the islands, many of the people I've met have become lifelong friends. I often think back to 'Tween Waters' sparse beginnings and fondly recall the early guests and the friends I made during those formative years of scraping and scratching to build the island getaway we all envisioned.

One of the earliest guests whom I'll never forget was Janice Culvert and her son, George. They hailed from Maryland, seeking refuge from George's allergies. He was a boy of twelve or thirteen when they first arrived, and they stayed for weeks or even months until his health improved. Year after year, they returned and saw 'Tween Waters transform from its weather-worn state into a burgeoning haven.

Janice's husband, Bob, was a true gem who embodied a spirit of humility and courage after surviving the terrible World War II siege at the Battle of the Bulge. The Culverts became more than just guests; they became like a second family, watching and supporting our growth as if it were their own.

When Janice passed, we planted a tree and placed a plaque in her honor. During his subsequent visits, Bob continued to serve as our de facto social ambassador, always making guests feel welcome. Their legacy lives on at 'Tween Waters, a testament to the power of human connection.

Another unforgettable guest was Harry Lamdon. He and his wife first stayed in a less-than-ideal room, but I promised Harry that better accommodations were on the horizon. True to my word, when we completed the new buildings on the bay in 1978, Harry was among the first to enjoy them. He continued to visit for six or seven years, becoming a cherished friend. His loyalty, kindness, and friendly face year after year helped sustain us in those early days.

Regular visitor Gene Truslow is also etched in my memory. Gene was a widower from Buffalo, New York, who sought solace in the warmth of our community and would book a three-month stay each winter. In January 1977, Gene and I sat alone in the dining room, the only two souls keeping the place from being a ghost town. That was a tough time. Truth be told, his staying with us was the only thing that prevented us from suffering a complete shutdown during that season. Those early days were lean, but they were rich with camaraderie and hope.

Gene's presence was a reminder of 'Tween Waters' potential, even when times said otherwise.

Other dear friends who helped make life a joy were Dave and Lynn "Lynnie" Garwood. Angie and I met Dave and Lynnie through Angie's work as a real estate agent. She had sold them a property at South Seas, and what started as an everyday professional relationship soon became a lasting friendship. Before long, we were spending regular time together, and we especially enjoyed fishing trips with them two or three times a year.

Our fishing guide for most of those outings was Jerry Way, a great guy who had moved with his family to Sanibel in the 1950s. Jerry became a legendary guide who worked out of our 'Tween Waters marina for nearly forty years. With his easygoing sense of humor and vast knowledge of the local waters, he quickly became part of our fun fishing adventures.

One tradition we had on these trips was taking turns bringing snacks, and it gradually turned into a bit of a competition—who could come up with the best nibbles? It finally came to the point where I wanted to really take things to the next level—a friendly raising of the stakes. So I hatched a plan that was, if I do say so myself, a stroke of genius. To pull it off, I hooked in the help of both Jerry and Chef Iggy, the head chef at 'Tween Waters at the time.

The idea was to start the day with, well, less-than-impressive snacks—really skimpy little crackers and finger foods and such. Then we'd spring the real surprise. Unfortunately, Lynnie couldn't make it that morning, but the plan was already in motion, and there was no turning back.

We left as the sun rose, and we were on the water behind Buck Key when Jerry suddenly spun and looked off the starboard bow.

"I hear a boat coming!" he yelled with a feigned urgency that was Oscar worthy. "They must be coming for our spot!" Any fishing guide worth his salt gets very protective of his prized "spots," where he knows fish hang out.

Well, Dave had just gotten one of the newfangled VHS camcorders—remember this was the eighties—and he loved to shoot footage. There was a boat racing at us like some sort of James Bond daredevil, so Dave grabbed his camera and started to film. He zoomed in. It was one of our 'Tween Waters rental boats, and... wait a minute! It was Chef Iggy! Decked in full chef whites! One hand mashed down his chef's cap against the roaring boat's headwind as he raced up with a... FLAMBÉ CART?!

Barely able to contain our laughter, we all sat down for fresh omelets, mimosas, and Bloody Marys as we floated on the tranquil waters of Pine Island Sound. It was a sight to behold and took flabbergasted Dave completely by surprise.

Back home a short time later, Lynnie asked him how the snacks were. "Meh," he said with a shrug, "they weren't much."

"Good," she replied. "I made breakfast."

That night, we all headed to the Garwoods' for a fish dinner, and the highlight was watching Lynnie's face when she saw the footage Dave had captured of our surprise, and we excitedly relived the gag together. Those were the kinds of days where laughter came easily, and good times seemed to stretch on forever. In the end, it wasn't about the fish we caught (or didn't catch), but the joy of creating tales we'd tell for years to come.

Speaking of which, if you should happen to see me around 'Tween Waters, be sure to ask about how the Garwoods later blew my culinary prank out of the water. Let's just say the sky was the limit!

The friends I made during this period were as diverse and colorful as the island itself. Remo, the plumber; Dan Burner, the architect; and Don Mayeron, who opened The Mucky Duck, were regulars at breakfast.

We'd sit around, sipping coffee and swapping stories. Dan was a character, always full of surprises. I remember one morning he arrived looking like he'd been through a barroom brawl. It turned out he had crash-landed his paraglider—a motorized hang glider—into the mangroves. Despite the mishap of being nearly ripped to pieces, Dan's adventurous spirit was undaunted and infectious, and his laughter brightened many mornings.

The Bubble Room, an iconic restaurant on Captiva, was founded by two of our early honeymoon guests, Katie Gardenia and Jamie Farquharson. Their vision and creativity transformed a simple idea into a beloved local treasure. Their story speaks to the magic of the island and the inspiration it sparks in those who visit.

In the early eighties, we also had a brush with Hollywood. One day, a man checked in, looking for a break from Miami. As we chatted, I discovered he was Don Johnson, filming the pilot for a new show called Miami Vice. His co-star, Edward James Olmos, often visited with his family. They were unassuming, down-to-earth people who found solace in the tranquility of the island. Their presence added a touch of glamour to our budding vacation destination.

The early years were marked by humble beginnings, the warmth of camaraderie and friendships, and the promise of a horizon still decades away. I often think about the many, many people—staff, visitors, and friends—who became integral threads in the tapestry of my innkeeper's tales. Their stories, interwoven into the history of 'Tween Waters, continue to inspire and shape the spirit of everything we do.

Six

Riding the Tourism Wave

As a rookie in the world of guest services, 'Tween Waters became my proving ground. I was barely in my thirties by the early 1980s, and what I lacked in formal training in the hospitality business, I worked like the dickens to make up for by running full throttle on enthusiasm and a can-do spirit. A prime example is our restaurant business, which I learned on-the-fly, with a generous topping of talented staff support and a healthy dollop of imagination.

Our food and dining operations became a cornerstone of our success during the late 1970s and early 1980s. Chef Tony was our first culinary leader. He was a super guy and a visionary in the kitchen. Key members of his team were Kitty Scott and Timmy Jardas, who started as a dishwasher on Christmas Day in 1976 and worked his way up. During his many years with us, I came to appreciate Timmy as a versatile team player because he filled so many positions. These dated from his time as the poolside bartender at our original No-See-Um Bar, to facilities management, to moving and arranging unit furniture, to his role in our dining operations. Conscientious and reliable, he contributed to our growth in countless ways with his hard work and dedication.

Establishing a reputation for excellent food became crucial to our early survival during the off-season when visitors slowed to a trickle. We had to devise a way our dining operation could help carry us through the summer doldrums and keep the hard-working staff's paychecks flowing.

The islands were nearly deserted of visitors when I pulled the team together for a brainstorming session, out of which came a thunderbolt of an idea: a signature dining event. What can bring together family, friends, fun, and food? A delicious Thanksgiving dinner as spectacular as our sunsets!

As our excitement mounted, we realized there was one small catch: we couldn't be sure the idea would fly. None of us had ever attempted such a remarkable dinner celebration before. It would be a matter of blind faith and a formidable test for us and Chef Tony. Pushing self-doubt aside, we pressed forward and prepared a scrumptious Thanksgiving meal.

And our spirits soared when they *did* come—and in droves! The restaurant was packed, with Chef Tony and his staff thrown into the proverbial fire. But we managed to pull it off.

I can't tell you how relieved I was, because that age-old adage is so true: You only get one chance to make a first impression! That inaugural Thanksgiving dinner was our culinary coming-out party. Bolstered by its success, we thought, "Hey, that worked!

Why not try Sunday brunch?!" So we fired up the kitchen and went to work.

I can still recall the sound of searing pans and clattering cookware in the bustling kitchen. Can still smell the savory aroma of sizzling bacon as it mingled with the voices of cooks and waitstaff filling orders like the precision team they were becoming, all while the dining room buzzed with lively chatter. Before long, our Sunday Brunch became a huge hit, and when the crowd topped 300 people, we knew we were on our way to establishing our second popular island event.

I had never been involved in serving so many meals before. The aftermath appeared as if an army had passed through and we had fed every single troop. This success helped us decide to keep the momentum going with a seafood buffet on Fridays during the tourist season, which also became tremendously popular.

To help develop our reputation and draw visitors and locals alike to 'Tween Waters, we became known for our welcoming holiday buffets. Here was a tasty arrangement for our Easter buffet.

These tradition-building events were crucial to our early development. Not only did they help establish us in the minds of seasonal visitors, but they also helped put us on the map during the off-season, when we built lasting friendships among our fellow islanders.

The boyhood lessons of my Italian family dinner traditions back in Rochester continued to ring true as I navigated these new waters of hospitality. Gathering for a meal is about much more than simply eating. Such a shared experience nurtures neighborly relationships and builds community.

These early off-season dinner events set the tone for a very special occasion we would host a few years later during the height of season. One night a week for fourteen weeks during season, Angie and I would transform the Old Captiva House's dining room into an experience straight out of a vintage Neapolitan tale: Italian buffet night.

We draped the tables with traditional red-and-white checkered cloths and decorated each table with a classic Chianti bottle for a candleholder, with the melting, tapered candle wax slowly marking the relaxed pace of the evening.

And the music. Of course, we had to have Italian music! From easy-listening to toe-tapping, I recall performances by Mario Lanza and Louis Prima for our delighted diners, and I can still hear Louie's raspy singing voice, which gave the entire room the air of a big Italian family gathering.

The resort managed to cover its operating costs back then, but not much more, so we couldn't pay for any extra help. But we didn't mind rolling up our sleeves together to make it a success.

In our heart of hearts, there was something special for us in bringing a piece of our shared roots, our Italian heritage, to life in our little slice of paradise—one scrumptious dish and perfectly paired bottle of wine at a time.

Authentic Italian cuisine is so much about the sensory experience, and what really hit you when you walked in was the mouthwatering aromas. The fragrant scent of garlic, of course, tickled your nose, along with the sweet tang of provolone cheese from a sixty-pound wheel I hung from the ceiling. That was quite a conversation piece!

Among the dishes we served were homemade manicotti wrapped in handcrafted crepes, eggplant Parmesan, chicken cacciatore, and pesce marinato. The antipasti spread served as a feast all on its own: sliced meats, marinated vegetables, olives, the works. And the desserts? *Buon appetito!* Guests enjoyed either spumoni or homemade cannoli, with shells I made myself.

The gatherings grew weekly as word spread until we were serving capacity crowds of 250 to 300 people each night. From the planning and the preparation to the cooking and the cleanup, it was exhausting work for the two of us, as I continued in my full-time role as the general manager of 'Tween Waters and Angie worked as a real estate agent.

I'll always remember one particularly crazy-busy night, when Angie and I barely had a moment to breathe. By the time we had finished cleaning up and turned out the lights, it was about one in the morning.

We decided to go for a walk on the beach to unwind when we got home. Strolling in a brisk onshore wind, we watched the Gulf churn under a full moon, as the waves rolled in and whitecaps danced on the glistening waters as far as we could see. The pulsing, silver-blue light of a large ship on the horizon flickered against the night sky as I drew a refreshing breath and exhaled my exhaustion.

We were tired, but it was the kind of tired you were proud and happy to have earned. It was great to be young and to feel deeply connected to each other and to something bigger than ourselves.

Angie and I hosted the Italian buffet for six years, but it eventually reached a point where we could no longer keep up with the demands of pulling it off at the level we had set for ourselves. When it came time to turn out the lights for the last time, I couldn't imagine bringing in someone else to take over. I was concerned it wouldn't be able to carry on with the personal and passionate commitment and care we had poured into it.

I still think fondly about the Italian buffet nights—of how Angie and I would savor the dining room as it came alive with the chatter and the laughter of guests and newly made friends, and with the smells, sights, and sounds of Italy.

We made so many wonderful friends during our Thanksgiving dinners, Sunday brunches, seafood buffets, and Italian buffets. They created considerable interest in our plucky little business as our reputation grew. People seemed genuinely elated to see us, the new kids on the block, taking such deep-seated pride in 'Tween Waters, demonstrating that we cared immensely about the quality of what we were doing.

I can't emphasize enough how important our early food and dining efforts were to our development. I'm truly indebted to Chef Tony for introducing me to the restaurant business. He had a fantastic personality for interacting with guests, and he loved to mingle and chat in the dining room, kind of like our gourmet ambassador. Such a friendly and welcoming spirit has become part of who we are.

That's not to say he didn't have his quirks. He could be cantankerous and hard to handle when the pressure mounted, especially around our holiday meals. I remember having to come in at three in the morning on Thanksgiving or Christmas to calm things down in the kitchen during preparations for the gala meal.

I'm on the right, planning our next big buffet event with Chef Tony, who was key to establishing our reputation for exceptional cuisine and warm hospitality. With two Tonys, I was given the nickname Boss Tony to avoid confusion.

But that was just a minor speed bump when I think about the breadth of Chef Tony's impact. He was so instrumental in our success. When he would take a day off, I would be the chef. So I learned how to cook breakfast for more than a hundred people.

It was a fascinating learning experience for me, to say the least. He taught me so much about the restaurant business. His lessons were invaluable, and I'm forever grateful for his guidance during these formative years.

Working with our restaurant staff taught me one of the most important lessons I've ever learned about humility and maintaining my composure. I was feeling a lot of pressure trying to ensure the restaurant was successful, and I wanted everything to be just right. When something went wrong one time after a trying evening shift, I lost my cool and launched into an expletive-laden rant, using language I should not have uttered.

The next day, I discovered that one of my young waitresses had quit because of my outburst. That rocked me to my core because I knew I could be better. I needed to get a grip, and I had to make amends. So I immediately called her on the phone.

"I'm terribly, terribly sorry," I said. "I had no right to speak the way I did and to lash out like that."

Then her father, who had been listening to our conversation, surprised me when he interrupted. "Listen, Tony," he said in a voice edged with a firm resolve. "We can accept your apology and understand how something like that can happen in the heat of the moment, but I don't think I want my young daughter working there any longer."

This was a wake-up call about my behavior that rocked me to my core. Number one, like a bolt from the blue, I realized I wasn't the most important person in the operation—not by a long shot. That honor belonged to the frontline staff. They were the ones who made everything happen.

You can have the best-laid plans, but if there aren't talented and dedicated people to carry them out, you're sunk. This episode taught me to fully appreciate and respect that. Secondly, as a leader, I understood I had to practice grace under pressure, no matter the circumstances.

Equally important, I realized my actions had a profound impact on those around me, and it was my responsibility to set the tone of our company culture, a role I've taken very seriously since that day.

That regrettable episode was among the growing pains we all experienced in our restaurant business, which grew rapidly, sometimes outstripping our ability to keep up. Chef Tony eventually left after five years, and I believe a big part of it was because he felt the increasing pressure of our expanding operations. But the foundation he helped lay was solid.

We were able to keep the restaurant open year-round, which was unusual back then, as most places shut down for a period of time after Easter. This was important to us because we wanted to be more than just a seasonal stop; we wanted to be a part of the islands' community fabric.

We stumbled a time or two along the way, but it was the spirit of teamwork and a shared commitment to excellence that got us through our fledgling food and dining years. We learned to roll with the punches, find humor in the chaos, and always strive to do our best—lessons that continue to guide me.

Seven

Learning to Listen

I'VE ALWAYS STRIVED TO exceed our visitors' expectations with unparalleled vacation experiences. And when I stop and think about it, my own personal interactions with the hospitality business as a customer—life on the *other* side of the reception desk—set the stage with insights I've carried over into my own professional life.

One such incident traces back to when I was just twenty-six years old and living as a newlywed with Angie in Rochester. This was before we decided to make the big move down to Sanibel.

It was our first anniversary, and we wanted to make it special by taking a trip to a nice hotel in Toronto. It was in March, nearing the end of my snowplow season, and Angie and I agreed Toronto would be a fun getaway. Her infectious smile at the prospect increased my anticipation of an unforgettable anniversary. Filled with excitement, we hopped in our car.

Heading west out of Rochester, we passed Buffalo and Niagara Falls before crossing into Canada over the Lewiston-Queenston Bridge that spans the Niagara River. That's when we saw the sign saying studded snow tires were banned in Ontario this time of year.

What?

Our hearts sank. We had no idea about this requirement; we still had our snow tires on because in Rochester their use extended past our March anniversary month. I pulled up to the Canadian side, and a pleasant border officer informed me that while we could continue, we risked being stopped and fined $150 every time law enforcement spotted us. They would literally be able to hear us coming, as studded tires make a distinct buzzing sound on the pavement.

Angie and I shared a moment of panic. An infraction totaling $150 a pop was a lot of money in our fledgling marriage. We were sitting in Canada with a set of illegal tires that could drain our bank account when all was said and done. Putting our heads together, we wondered what we could do. I could see the frustrated hopelessness in her eyes when she suggested scrapping the whole trip, but I didn't want to ruin our anniversary plans, which included flowers waiting in the room.

She became teary but remained determined to see our plan through when we formulated a workaround solution. We drove the nearly 200 miles back to Rochester and swapped my car with the studded snow tires for my mother's vehicle, which was mounted with regular-season tires. (Mom was in Florida during this time helping Dad with his Parkinson's.)

Swapping our luggage from one car to the other, we set off again. What should have been a three-hour drive had turned into a nine-hour ordeal—not a great way to mark your first year of marriage. When we finally arrived at the Sutton Place Hotel in Toronto, I was frustrated because I felt like the hotel had dropped the ball with a lack of anticipation for its guests' needs.

As I pulled to a stop, an attendant came out to greet us. "Good day, and welcome to Sutton Place. May I park your car?"

I gave the guy a casual wave. "Not just yet, thanks." A plan percolating in my mind, I walked inside and met with a very nice front desk clerk. "May I please see the manager?"

The manager came out, and I explained in a friendly manner what had happened because of our snow tires. "Jeez," I said, shrugging my shoulders and plaintively lifting my hands, "when I called in my reservation, your staff member took my address, so she knew we were coming from the States. Wouldn't it have been a good idea for her, as a guest courtesy, to mention that studded snow tires are banned in Ontario this time of year?"

The manager's brow furrowed for a second. "You know, that's a great idea. I'll see that we make that notification part of our reservation information."

"Well, that's fantastic for all your future visitors, but," I continued with a slight grin, "what about us? Is there anything you can do? Not having that information cost us considerable time and money, and you only have one first anniversary."

He gave me a nodding smile, seeing right through my "what have you done for me lately" act. "Tell you what," he said. "We're going to give you complimentary parking and free continental breakfast for your two days with us."

I thought that was a very nice offer. As we checked into our room, I mulled over the fact that the manager's response was a smart one. It was a goodwill gesture, and it did the trick by making us feel valued. And maybe most important of all, it made us feel as if we had been *heard*. The manager had listened to our concern and suggested a solution.

When it comes to interactions in everyday life, not just in hospitality, we all want to feel valued and heard. Was the snow tire snafu entirely the hotel's fault? No. I was probably partly responsible, too. But they took ownership of their shortcoming in the eyes of a guest and offered a fix.

This customer service interaction clicked with me, and I must have tucked it away in my memory because I recalled it after I entered the hospitality business. I emphasize with our staff how important it is for our customers to feel heard and valued because it validates their concerns, fosters trust, and demonstrates that their satisfaction is a priority. It's more than simply resolving an issue; it's making certain guests feel respected and appreciated, which ultimately enhances their overall experience and perception of us. And that is so important.

Some years later, after I'd been running 'Tween Waters for a year or two and was still learning the finer points of guest relations, another situation popped up. Angie and I took a vacation to Las Vegas. We're not big gamblers by any means, but we'd been working hard and wanted to squeeze in some time off with a change of scenery.

The old maxim that the house always wins in Vegas may hold true for the casinos, but customers can come out on top, too—if they know how to get there. One day, I was out playing golf and met a fellow golfer named Bob, a car salesman from Pennsylvania. He was a spitfire of a guy and really gregarious. We shared some laughs and had a good time on the links.

Afterward, we thought it would be fun to get together with our wives over dinner and see a show. It turned out, both Angie and Bob's wife had their hearts set on seeing Engelbert Humperdinck sing at the Westgate Las Vegas Resort & Casino, where he'd been headlining in neon style with songs such as "Release Me" and "Spanish Eyes." A real crooner in that classic Vegas style, Engelbert's actual name is Arnold Dorsey. But he adopted the stage name Engelbert Humperdinck, after the German composer known for the opera *Hansel and Gretel*. Go figure.

Back then, you bought admission tickets, but you didn't get a seat assignment; that was taken care of at the door. And by "taken care of"—again, in classic Vegas style—it was understood that you slipped the doorman a nice tip in exchange for a primo seat assignment.

I paid what I thought was a generous gratuity because I wanted to get close to the stage so Angie could really enjoy a memorable show. Imagine our disappointment when the usher marched us all up to the nosebleed seats. Jeez. From up in the rafters, we wouldn't be seeing Mr. Humperdinck—we'd be seeing Mr. Humperdinky!

Gazing around from our seats, Bob and I exchanged a confused glance.

"Tony?" he said. "Did you tip the door guy?"

"Plenty."

He frowned. "Yeah, I gave him a nice tip, too." He paused for a moment and I could practically see the gears turning in his head.

"Wait here," he said. "I'll be right back."

A spry guy, he bounded down the stairs from our perch in the stratosphere to the lower section. An usher stopped him and asked if he could help. Bob gave him a smile and said, "Nothing personal, but I don't wanna speak to the angels. I wanna speak to God."

The usher understood that Bob wanted to talk with whoever was in charge, not their assistants, someone at the "top of the heap" as Sinatra used to belt out. Bob cordially talked to the manager, and boom, all of a sudden, we're sitting in the front row for Engelbert Humperdinck!

What had happened here? It became clear that Bob wanted to ensure his concerns were being addressed by someone with authority. A decision-maker. When I returned to 'Tween Waters after our getaway, it sank in that when guests are unhappy, they often just want to speak to someone who can make right a perceived wrong.

Oftentimes, the heart of the matter isn't the initial problem. For guests, it's feeling like they're being treated fairly. It's human nature. Many times, when a visitor comes to our front desk and wants to see a manager or the owner, it's not because the front desk staff isn't doing their job. It's because the guest wants to talk to God, the highest level, so to speak—not the angels.

These experiences stayed with me as I built my career in hospitality. Making guests feel heard and valued can turn a potential disaster into a positive experience.

At 'Tween Waters, I make it a point to be available for guests. To assure them they're speaking to someone in charge. It's not that the front desk staff or others working to assist visitors aren't capable. In fact, it's not about *us* at all. It's about our *guests* knowing we value them enough that we make our top people available to genuinely listen to them and help them.

Generating smiles and memorable experiences is at the heart of everything we're about. Whether offering a complimentary breakfast or upgrading a room, these small gestures of goodwill made guests feel valued and respected. And that, I believe, is a cornerstone of great hospitality.

Eight

The Crow's Nest Takes Flight

IN THE EARLY 1980S, we embarked on one of the most ambitious projects I had ever tackled—building the Crow's Nest restaurant. It was 1981, and the island was still a relatively quiet and somewhat undiscovered little beach town community. There wasn't as much steady demand to fill our rooms as there is today, so we had to get creative and figure out other ways to supplement our revenue and build our visibility as a destination.

The first thing we had to do to make room for the Crow's Nest was reconfigure the property. We picked up and moved what was then the manager's quarters—a pudgy, unassuming building on a concrete slab where the restaurant is now located—to a spot around back, behind the kitchen.

As the establishment took shape, the old Jerry Lee Lewis song "Great Balls of Fire" kept playing through my mind because the Crow's Nest featured an astonishing fireplace. This signature element wasn't just any old ho-hum hearth; it was a commanding centerpiece for the entire restaurant.

Of course, we needed truckloads of wood to feed it, and I think I'm probably responsible for incinerating most of the Australian pine on Captiva. Those trees, which arrived in Florida in the late 1800s from Australia and the South Pacific, are an invasive species known to overtake indigenous trees and plants.

They also have very shallow root systems, and they topple in strong storm winds. In fact, for decades, the towering, long-needle trees had formed a signature look along Captiva Drive—until they met their match in 2004, when Hurricane Charley leveled them with sustained winds of 150 mph, forever changing the landscape.

An Australian pine's wood can be hard as iron. If you cut the tree when it's dry, sparks fly off a chainsaw. So we would cut it when it was still green and then let it dry, and it became fantastic for our fireplace, where it flamed beautifully, much to the delight of our customers.

How key was that hearth to our early eighties growth? Well, it kind of took on a life of its own and launched a Crow's Nest tradition. Every Thanksgiving, we'd kindle up a comfy fire and keep it crackling until nearly Easter.

The welcoming venue became well-known and was a big draw, especially on those chilly, rainy winter days and evenings when the winds blew and people needed a place to warm up and sip a cozy cocktail. Our "Great Balls of Fire" hearth wasn't simply part of the decor; it was essential to the experience, and it attracted folks from all over.

Along with the Crow's Nest, we also built two duplexes. Originally, each featured two bedrooms, making for a total of four. We named them after popular local sportfish: the Snook, Snapper, Pompano, and Redfish.

But in 2004, we renovated them when we realized the two-bedroom units would be way more in demand if they also offered two bathrooms. So we essentially split the duplexes in half—one side became a two-bedroom/two-bath unit, and the other side a one-bedroom suite.

It turned out to be a great decision and their popularity soared. Even though those units weren't historic, like some of the others, they offered a better view of the Gulf. Being up five or six steps gave them enough elevation to see over the road and out to the water.

The Crow's Nest was a new concept for us. It was built to be a public restaurant, very warm and cordial, and a touch different. We had these really cool booths and tables, and the entire floor was oak. My cousins, who had a hardwood flooring business up in Rochester, shipped all the wood down and laid it themselves.

The dance floor was a beautiful parquet. With all the stomping, gliding, and sliding, it took a beating over the years, but it held up like a champ. We've since been through a number of beautiful remodels, but... I've always had a soft spot for the original Crow's Nest. It was a unique rendezvous where people gathered over good times, especially in those early years when Captiva was still a sleepy hideaway.

The Crow's Nest wasn't just about the building, though—it was about the people who made it what it was. I had some young folks working for me back then who were instrumental in our success. Kitty Scott, for instance, ran our dining room. She was a young lady who wouldn't let anything stand in her way. She attended school while working for us and became a hospice nurse. To me, that's a special calling and takes a special kind of person, and it shows the wonderful woman she is. She's still helping so many people and families today with her caregiving and positive energy.

My go-to guy, Timmy Jardas, made his presence felt in so many ways. He had started out running the No-See-Um pool bar back in our sandspur days, but eventually worked his way up through many varied positions to become the Crow's Nest manager. He loved the entertainment aspect, and what he did to help the good times roll was nothing short of astonishing. While room bookings hit some slumps in those days, Timmy was instrumental in keeping the Crow's Nest hopping.

Then there was Dan Kinsley. He came on to run the Crow's Nest after we promoted Timmy to a food and beverage manager. Dan marked his fortieth year with us in 2024. A terrific guy, he works primarily at banquets and the morning shift. And I can't forget Robert L, a retired police officer who overcame a lot in his life and helped with accounting. He became such a good friend. I enjoyed working with him, and he was a great part of the team.

One of the keys to our success in crafting the Crow's Nest into a hopping entertainment hub was converting the old manager's quarters into a band house. And I mean literally. We housed touring musical bands.

Timmy brought in acts from all over the place. Among the memorable ones were the Scallion Sisters, a female rock group out of Atlanta that drew huge crowds; and The Modulators, a party band from Cincinnati, Ohio, who vacationed and played for about two weeks.

Then there was Dr. Hector and the Groove Injectors, a rock'n'roll band, with soul and rhythm and blues thrown in for good measure. Their leader, guitarist Dru Lombar, had shared stages with the likes of The Allman Brothers, The Charlie Daniels Band, and Lynyrd Skynyrd. If guitar amps were designed to go to ten, theirs were set on twelve! They were nuts, but everybody loved them.

On the other side of the musical spectrum, I can't leave out John Solman and Andy Mayo, a fantastic duo. John later became a solo piano entertainer, and I remember covering a shift in the lounge one night while I was also the resort's general manager. John played for two and a half hours straight, singing the whole time. He knew how to connect with a crowd like nobody else.

John Soloman (left) and Andy Mayo were a fantastic musical duo. John later went solo as a piano player and singer.

The Crow's Nest helped us become known for bringing visitors and locals alike together to share a good time. Up to this point, we had experienced a nice winning streak with events like our Sunday Brunch and a seafood buffet, and we decided if a few fun events were good, more celebrations would be even better! This is how we came up with the outlandish concept of hosting an Oktoberfest.

I have to hand it to Lloyd; it was his original idea. October was always a slow month—occupancy rates on the islands would drop to around twenty or thirty percent, so we needed something to draw people in. Something big. Lloyd looked at me one day and said, "Let's put on an Oktoberfest!"

When we hosted Oktoberfest for eighteen years straight, it was all hands on deck for the staff, who embraced the festive spirit.

There I was, an Italian guy, and I didn't know the first thing about hosting an authentic Oktoberfest. We needed to dive in and learn how to do it right. There was a restaurant up in Rochester that hosted a fantastic Oktoberfest every year, so we sent Timmy up there to do a little research.

After he came back, we planned everything out, down to the smallest detail. The old TV show, *The Love Boat,* was in its heyday and we all felt a kinship with the show's cruise director Julie, who was responsible for throwing these large, ocean-going events and coordinating themed activities.

And while our Oktoberfest was all about celebrating German culture, food and beverage, we couldn't do it right without the music. It was Timmy to the rescue.

He brought in a band called the Stratton Mountain Boys, an Austrian musical group based in Vermont. These guys weren't just any band. They had played at the opening of the Germany Pavilion at Disney's Epcot Center—that's how fantastic and in-demand they were all over the country.

(From left) Yours Truly, Timmy, Chef Iggy, and Kitty grab a fun stage photo during a break in the Stratton Mountain Boys show.

After landing what was considered the Dream Team Oktoberfest band, we erected a mammoth tent, built an inviting courtyard, and laid down a big dance floor and a stage. The whole place looked like a scene out of a German postcard. I remember thinking, "Well, this is either going to be a huge success or we're going to fall flat on our face."

But when we opened that evening, the place was packed. We had everything—the great music and dancing, the sausages, schnitzel, beer, schnapps, you name it. We even converted one of the cottages into a makeshift beer hall, with kegs lined up wall to wall.

I was so heartened to see how much people loved it and really got into the festival spirit. Saturday nights, we drew about a thousand people. This was years before Cape Coral started its Oktoberfest, so we were the first ones in Southwest Florida to do anything like it. People showed up in limos and in big groups, flocking in from all over and ready to have a good time.

In order to get the permit required to serve alcohol at the festival, we needed to find a charitable organization to whom we could donate a portion of the proceeds as a fundraiser of sorts, and we selected the United Way.

Later on, we developed a program that consisted of an employee campaign where we provided our staff the opportunity to deduct whatever they felt they could from their paychecks, and we matched it dollar for dollar. This program is still in place, and there have been years where our folks have contributed as much as $15,000, and the company has matched that. I can't tell you how proud I am of the company and our employees for this effort.

Additionally, I joined the board of directors of the United Way of Lee, Hendry, and Glades Counties to help advance its mission. I'm still on the board all these years later, in addition to serving as the fundraising campaign chair for Sanibel and Captiva. We've always made it a priority to support the United

Way, and I see the company and our employees remaining strong on that front in the future.

The United Way is such a wonderful service organization, and I believe each of us should embody a personal commitment to service as a way to give back to the community we call home. In fact, there is a favorite quote of mine by Muhammad Ali: "Service to others is the rent you pay for your room here on Earth." For me, that sums it up very well.

Lloyd was instrumental as a mentor in philanthropy for me, and our company continues to support many of our non-profits on the islands. These include the Bailey-Matthews National Shell Museum & Aquarium, the Clinic for the Rehabilitation of Wildlife (CROW), F.I.S.H. of SanCap, the Sanibel-Captiva Conservation Society (SCCF), and the J.N. "Ding" Darling Wildlife Society, to name a few.

We hosted Oktoberfest for eighteen years straight, and when the fall came along, it was the place to be on the island, something people would look forward to every year—including our staff! We all dressed in traditional Bavarian costumes. Everybody's Irish on St. Patrick's Day, the old saying goes. From what I saw, everyone was German on Oktoberfest, too.

But the fun didn't stop with the *oompah-oompah* thigh-slapping of Oktoberfest. After we wrapped that up, we rolled right into Halloween. It was a natural: we already had the cavernous tent and courtyard set up, so we threw huge costume parties. We'd bring in a band, polish up the dance floor, and let the fun begin.

Our Halloween parties grew larger and larger every year, proving Southwest Florida's grapevine was alive and well. The bashes attracted a sea of revelers in costumes, with the music blaring and everyone dancing the night away. We'd have costume contests, and the cleverness and creativity that people showed were out of this world.

Costumed merrymakers and pranksters from near and far gathered for good times at our annual Halloween Party.

Two groups in particular I'll never forget. One was a gang who came dressed as the Titanic. Two people were sections of the ship, split in half, while another two were icebergs. Plus three or four others dressed as survivors, wrapped in life preservers, with white powder on their faces to look like they were floating in the icy water. They were fantastic!

Another one was a guy who came dressed as a famous chef, with an entourage in tow. One person dressed as the bottom half of a hamburger bun, another as the top bun, and in between, there was cheese, lettuce, and tomato—all portrayed by people in costumes. Every time the chef blew his whistle, the bottom bun would leap to the ground, and the rest would jump on to assemble the burger. It was hilarious, and people just howled!

But as the years rolled on, things started to change. Safety issues while driving became a bigger concern, and other party events started popping up in the area. It got to the point where we couldn't draw the same crowds to Oktoberfest and the Halloween bash like we used to. So, eventually, it made sense to quiet things down.

Still, the early eighties was a time when the Crow's Nest became a hub of activity, beyond the big festivals and holiday blowouts. Whether it was a cozy evening by the fireplace or a packed dance floor on a Saturday night with people lined up out the door, it was a place where people came together for good times and left with stories they'd tell for years to come.

Early in the evenings, there were mostly in-house guests or tourists staying somewhere on the islands, but the late-night crowd was mostly employees from other restaurants on the islands—places like The Bubble Room, The Mucky Duck, and the old Timmy's Nook, which was later rebuilt as The Green Flash. The working crowd would rush over after closing up to unwind with some fun and wouldn't leave until we turned the lights up at 1:45 a.m.

Timmy wanted to keep the entertainment momentum going and headed up our famous crab racing events, a quirky laugh riot that became a beloved tradition! Believe it or not, he ended up making a career out of it, traveling to compete in other competitions and to visit crab racing conventions. Budweiser even flew him out to California for a two-week event.

Around the same time, he was about to get married, and I've often wondered what the conversation with his future in-laws must have been like. I picture Timmy sitting across the dinner table from the man who's about to see his daughter settle into her life with her betrothed, and the inevitable question comes up.

"So, Timmy," his future father-in-law says, "what do you do for a living?"

I can just imagine the pregnant pause and the look on Timmy's face before he responds with that classic grin of his. "I race crabs."

The father of the bride shoots her mother an uneasy sidelong glance. This is when Timmy would reassure them with his famous quip: "Don't worry. They're not just your typical jumpers. These are *thoroughbred racers.*"

That was Timmy—quick with a line and always ready with a laugh. But what made him truly special was how he took something as simple as crab racing and turned it into a twenty-five-year phenomenon at 'Tween Waters, during which he saw generations of families come through. He had this incredible ability to remember names and faces, year after year. People came back just to see him, to be part of this offbeat little tradition he'd built.

When the global pandemic shut everything down for what seemed like an eternity, Timmy took a step back and decided to retire, and I knew it was the end of an era. He had thought about winding things down slowly, but Covid sealed the deal. Everything came to a sudden stop—and with it, our crustacean capers.

It was a tough decision to end the event, but I think it was a smart move to let the crab races skitter off into the history books and not attempt to find a replacement for Timmy. He left behind an unforgettable legacy of laughter and happiness, and trying to fill those shoes would've been impossible. Some things are better left as cherished memories for those who were lucky enough to be there.

Nine

Hijinx Hall of Fame

Big crowds and loads of laughter are certainly one way to create lasting memories, but it doesn't always take throngs of revelers to leave a lasting impression. In fact, one visitor created an entire scrapbook of memories all by himself. Let's just call the escapade worthy of the 'Tween Waters Hijinks Hall of Fame. I still laugh whenever I tell this story because you just can't make this stuff up!

For the longtime staff here—and there a quite a few—all you have to do is mention the name Aldo, and we're immediately transported back to a spiraling episode that seemed straight out of a caper comedy.

Back in the early eighties, we checked people in without taking a credit card; they simply settled their bill when they checked out. This is where Aldo, from Santiago, Chile, enters the story. He roared in like a daredevil in his silver-streak Datsun 280Z fastback and booked a room in the Seagrape building, overlooking Captiva Drive and the sparkling Gulf.

It didn't take long before he became the talk of the staff. With his stylish dark hair, olive-toned complexion, and hyper air of confidence, he had a certain swagger. The way he walked. The way he talked. In his mid-twenties, he projected an aura of being a man of international intrigue.

I was helping to cover the Crow's Nest lounge on the night when he staggered in, three sheets to the wind, and announced he was here to play with the band onstage.

"Well, Aldo," I said with a grin to let him down easy, "you really can't do that. The band has to kind of invite you onstage to play. That's how it works."

That apparently didn't sit well with the aspiring pop star. He stormed out to his 280Z, grabbed the guitar he had with him, and smashed it to bits right on the spot. Then, for reasons I still don't understand, he stumbled back into the lounge and threw me his car keys, as if to say, "There! Take that!"

Earlier that evening, my staff had told me he'd been buying Dom Perignon champagne like a drunken sailor and charging it to his room—at about $100 a bottle, that was a lot of expensive drinking. And one heckuva room tab in a period of about six hours for a guy who said he planned to stay for a week.

The next day, halfway sober and bleary-eyed, Aldo marched up to me with a demand. "Mr. Tony?" he said with a nod of his chin, full of bravado. "Mr. Tony Lapi?"

"Yes. How can I help you?"

He put his hands on his hips and declared, "I would now like you to return me my car keys."

"Well, I'd love to do that," I told him. "And here's the deal. I'll give your keys back when you pay your bill at checkout."

"What?" he sputtered. "You can't hold my car hostage." Jabbing his finger in my direction, he took a step toward me. "I'll call the sheriff."

"That's a great idea. Let's call the sheriff. In fact, I'll call him for you."

Of course, I knew the sheriff on our beat. When he arrived, Aldo and I told our sides of the story. Afterward, the sheriff took me aside. "Look, Tony, you really can't keep his keys because he's not actively trying to skip out on his tab at two in the morning or anything."

Yeah, right, I thought. *He's not trying to skip out YET.*

I thanked the sheriff and told him I'd think it over. And I decided I wasn't going to give Aldo his keys back unless and until he paid his mounting room tab. Scouting around, I found him on the beach.

"Listen, Aldo. Here's what we're going to do," I explained. "When you sit down for breakfast, I'm going to have breakfast with you. You sit down for lunch, and I'm going to have lunch with you. I'm going to be your constant companion for the rest of your stay, and you're not going to keep running up your room tab buying buckets of champagne."

"You can't do that!" he insisted.

"Yes, I can."

"I'm calling my lawyer!"

"Great! Give me his number, and I'll call him."

He scribbled out the number of his Miami lawyer and slapped the crinkled piece of paper into my palm. When I called his legal representative and said I had a "situation" with his client, I heard him sigh when I mentioned Aldo's name. By the tone of his voice, I could almost see him roll his eyes. He might as well have said, "Oh crap, what's he done this time?"

I explained Aldo had been running up a huge bill. I told him I had his car keys and didn't plan on giving them back until he paid what he owes.

"Look, Mr. Lapi," the attorney said, "I understand your situation. *Believe me,* I do." There was an eye roll in his tone again. "Send me all the charges, and I'll pay it. You have my word."

Wow, I said to myself. *Aldo has an attorney at his beck and call who is ready to pay for whatever straits he gets himself into?*

At any rate, the lawyer sounded reasonable and forthcoming, so I agreed. And that's when things got really wacky. The next thing I know, I get a call from Santiago, Chile. It was Aldo's mother, wailing in my ear and imploring me to let her son go!

I've never been known as a guy who's at a loss for words, but I was flabbergasted. First, he had dragged his lawyer into the fray, and now he was pulling in his mom as the official deal CLOSER?!

Jeez. I mean, I wasn't keeping the guy captive. He was free to leave whenever he wanted... with one small snag: not with his car until we settled up. Plain and simple.

I sensed Aldo rarely, if ever, heard "no" for an answer and was riding a wave of stubborn, short-fused desperation. It all boiled down to two important questions: Which one of us was going to blink first in our standoff? And what would he do next?

Whatever it was he might have up his sleeve, I was bound and determined that it wasn't going to be him somehow hot-wiring his 280Z so he could make a run for it without paying.

As I tossed things around in my mind, I realized I couldn't exactly post an around-the-clock guard to watch the car. My mind kept working... *around the clock... around the clock*. And then it hit me like a thunderbolt: "Rock Around the Clock"! That was it! That Bill Haley & His Comets tune that was featured in the classic 1970s film *American Graffiti*! The George Lucas movie inspired an action plan as my imagination ran wild.

Okay, maybe a little *too* wild.

I pulled together a handful of staff members and revealed my scheme. With Aldo's car parked nose-first under the Seagrape building, we scampered over with a tow chain and secured the front axle to one of the structural pilings, similar to how a young Richard Dreyfuss, out to prove his mettle, did to the cop cruiser in the movie.

I knew we had to move fast—before I talked myself out of such a zany move. We buried the chain in the sand so Aldo wouldn't see it if he managed to get the car started and tried to skip out on his bill.

Sure enough, a few hours later, Aldo hurried into his car, ripped the dashboard apart, and hot-wired the ignition. I heard the engine roar to life and hightailed it to his unit.

He looked up at me from the driver's seat as I hustled to his door and looked down at him. "Well, Mr. Tony Lapi," he said with a smirk, "I am now leaving, and you can do nothing to stop me."

I raised my eyebrows. "Well, you might wanna know that I chained your front axle to the building, and you're going to look awful dumb trying to drag it down Captiva Drive, not to mention across the bridge at Blind Pass."

His eyes narrowed, and we exchanged locked stares, like a pair of Western gunfighters at high noon. I knew he was trying to figure out if I was bluffing, and I waited for him to make the next move.

His unflinching gaze drilled into mine as he put the car in reverse and started to back up. I glanced at the chain as it slowly emerged from the sand like some kind of unfurling, steel sea snake. I gave him a final warning. "I wouldn't if I were you."

He dismissed me with a wave of his hand. "You are not me, Mr. Tony Lapi."

The car crept backward until the chain reached its full length. *Thunk.* The low-slung sports car stopped in its tracks. This was now a test of wills, and I could barely suppress a half grin.

Undaunted, Aldo pressed his foot harder on the gas pedal, and the rear tires started to spin as the car strained against the chain. He gave it more gas, his hands in a white-knuckled grip around the steering wheel. The tires began to spin faster and sink into the white sand, digging their own graves.

He juiced the RPMs, and the engine growled louder. His whirling tires sank lower. And lower. And lower. Disappearing into the sand until his rear bumper rested on the ground. He sat in the driver's bucket seat at about a twenty-degree upward-facing angle and stared straight ahead. The veins in his neck seemed to bulge in furious frustration.

When he slowly turned to look up at me, I lifted my hands in a calming gesture. "I'm working on straightening this all out with your attorney, and then we'll take the chain off."

He let loose a guttural moan and pounded his bedraggled dashboard until a wire somewhere came loose and the chugging engine sputtered and shut off.

Before walking back to the office, I gave the roof a friendly tap. "I'm sure you'll be outta here in no time."

Sure enough, the next day, I reached an agreement with his Miami lawyer and unchained the car. And our international man of intrigue drove off into the sunset, down Captiva Drive with the dashboard practically in his lap and wires flinging around like the spindly legs of a giant bug.

A couple of days later, a check showed up from Miami to pay Aldo's room tab, which totaled nearly $2,000—the equivalent of more than $6,000 today. I wondered how much Aldo would have to shell out to get his dashboard fixed, and I was certainly glad nobody got hurt. Other than the damage he did to his own dashboard, there was no major property damage, either. But it sure made for one heckuva tale. For both of us!

Ten

Good Times and a Near Miss

IN THE MID-1980S, WE set out to expand the Wakefield Room to maximize the square footage so we could host large events. There was a buzz of excitement surrounding the reimagining of what this venue could offer guests, especially with the planned stunning sunset views overlooking the Gulf. Lloyd had worked with the architect during the planning stages, and a pile driver to set the foundation pilings was scheduled to arrive in a week. Everything was a go.

But a little voice inside planted a seed of worry. Going all the way back to my boyhood days working on projects around our family home, I had always been a "measure twice/cut once" kind of guy. When you only have one shot at something, you better get it right the first time.

To this day, I don't know what it was, but I was driven by an overwhelming impulse to take a final look at the blueprints, specifically the two-dimensional elevation, which included, among other things, the various visual aspects and measurements. Lloyd, already satisfied with the prep, didn't think it was necessary to revisit old ground. Well, his old ground was new ground to me.

With the blueprints in hand and sweat dripping down my back, I rigged a stepladder on the top of my tractor's engine cowling and started up the rungs. Steadying myself on the wobbly contraption, the cowling supporting me flexed slightly and jolted me a bit off-balance—I counted my lucky stars OSHA wasn't around.

Regaining my footing, I mumbled to myself, "Jeez, Tony. What the hell are you doing? You're not a circus acrobat." Even though it felt like that sometimes.

Undeterred, I backhanded the sweat from my eyes and climbed one more rung, allowing me to see from the height indicated on the blueprint's elevation.

And that's when I nearly fell off the step labeled in screaming red: This Is Not a Step! From my vantage point, and stabilizing myself against the ladder's top cap as it dug into my shins, I stared directly into the roofs of the four cottages in front of where the redesigned Wakefield Room would be; there was absolutely no view of the Gulf for guests! There would be no gorgeous sunsets! No magical green flashes!

With visions of disaster dancing in my head, my heart hammered my rib cage as I scrambled down the ladder and rushed off to avoid a catastrophe. It was a matter of last-second luck and a pair of bruised shins that I caught the mistake in time.

We immediately halted the project and redesigned the structure, adding an additional seven-and-a-half feet to the building. This provided the water view we had dreamed of. Calamity avoided. *Whew!* That was a lesson in listening to your gut, the value of fresh eyes, and not taking anything for granted.

Once the Wakefield Room was completed, it became a striking and versatile space for meetings, wedding receptions, and a variety of other functions. For the first four years, though, we lacked an elevator, meaning everyone got their step exercises in!

Two visiting groups during this period stand out in my memory: the Women's Wellness Group and the Cracker Fishing Tournament. Talk about two crowds that were poles apart! Imagine a refined and reflective symphony experience crashing headlong into a blaring pedal-to-the-metal rock concert. We had the good sense to schedule them on different dates.

The driving force behind the Women's Wellness Group was a Captiva woman named Boots Freeman and her husband, Jim, who were originally from Cleveland. She had participated in such a group up in Ohio, and she thought it would be a great idea to replicate a wellness retreat on the island.

For over twenty years, this event drew as many as sixty women together, hosting a variety of activities and events, such as yoga sessions, tennis instruction, and massage therapists, with a focus on nutrition and whole life balance. Set amid the island's natural beauty, the gatherings provided a supportive space for women to share experiences as it fostered a sense of empowerment and community.

It was all about healthy, active living. And I can't forget the specialty health food menus—our kitchen staff had quite the workout of their own keeping up with those, as in driving them up the walls!

I always had to chuckle when I'd see some of the participants quietly slipping into Crow's Nest later in the evenings for cheeseburgers and fries. Who could blame them? They were delicious! Despite the kitchen's moaning and groaning over the group's special menu, it was a remarkable event that became a staple of our offerings.

Then there was the Cracker Fishing Tournament. Now, that was a horse—er, I mean fish—of a different color. The tournament deeply strengthened our ties to Fort Myers and all Southwest Florida, thanks to the efforts of Sam Galloway Jr. and Wesley Hanson, who reminded me of Paul Bunyon. He stood about six-seven and topped the scale at about 300 pounds, but he could dance like a ballerina. They met as students at Fort Myers High School in the 1960s.

Sam was such a great guy as both a successful businessman and a community philanthropist. His local family roots stretched back to 1927, when his grandparents arrived in Fort Myers. They bought a car dealership called Lee Motors, later renamed Sam Galloway Ford in 1963, the same year the Sanibel Causeway opened. Taking over the family business in 1971 at the age of twenty-seven, Sam became the youngest Ford dealer in the United States at that time.

We hosted the Cracker Fishing Tournament, which became a signature event and was noted for its boisterous spirit, rich traditions, and enough fish stories to fill a flats boat. Living up to the tournament's name, these guys embodied the old cracker spirit.

The term "cracker" generally describes early Florida cattle ranchers who "cracked" leather whips in the air to drive their herds. Think Indiana Jones, only with cowboy hats instead of a fedora.

One such prominent "cracker" with local ties from the mid-1800s was Jake Summerlin, a pioneering rancher whose operation would drive cattle to docks where the Punta Rassa boat ramp is today at the mainland foot of the causeway. There they were loaded on ships bound for Key West, Cuba, and the West Indies. Summerlin Road, a major thoroughfare in Fort Myers, is named after him.

The guys who participated in the tournament embodied the old crackers' reputation for... let's say, their rambunctious tendencies. Quiet reserve was in short supply, and no fish story was too outrageous.

All in all, however, they were a fun-loving crew whose bark was worse than their bite. But they could eat, drink, and party like nobody's business, and they taught me a thing or two. I learned how to roast a whole hog and make cabbage-palm fritters that were so delicious, your taste buds would throw a party!

The tournament kicked off with a shotgun start right from our marina, and the boats roared down the Roosevelt Channel, hell-bent for Pine Island Sound in search of snook, redfish, snapper, and other sport fish. (Local flavor tidbit: old-timers will tell you the correct pronunciation of the word "snook" rhymes with "Luke," not "look.")

The tourney's banquet schedule was legendary. Thursday nights were prime rib, and the anglers could eat an astounding amount. Fridays featured the hog roast with those unforgettable cabbage-palm fritters. Saturdays, participants would fry up their catch, while the Sunday banquet was New York strip.

If the event's banquets were the stuff of legend, one local band that kept the party popping was just as memorable. More than thirty years later, I'm still friends with Doug Simonds, who blew a mean trumpet for a high-energy group called Unicorn Run. They served up a blend of rock, pop, and funk that had the Crow's Nest soaring until nearly two a.m.

But the fun didn't always stop there. On some nights, the band would set up at the pool area after last call, where the music might go on until the first rays of dawn. Often fueled by generous tips from tournament anglers who wanted to keep the good times rolling, those late-night jams had ears ringing long after the last notes faded.

Despite the madcap mischief of it all, the tourney participants fished all day in the September heat. Their tenacious stamina and ability to operate on little sleep was astonishing.

Those tournament times were as fun as they were wild, and our staff wasn't afraid to get in on the tomfoolery. One year, Timmy Jardas, living in employee housing, decided to have a bit of fun with his fellow staff members who also lived on-site.

After the hog roast, the employees had a house party, and he wedged the beast's head inside one of the bathroom toilet bowls. There it sat under the closed lid. It gazed up like a charred demon as it waited for one of our unsuspecting female staff members with its bronzed and blackened eyes, its mouth a frightening grimace of jagged tusks.

The old employee housing building was the site of quite a few staff pranks over the years.

We got a boatload of laughs imagining one of the ladies, a few Rum Runners over the line, lifting the lid, only to be met by that ferocious sight! The women who lived in employee housing were wonderful and knew how to take a prank as well as pull one themselves, so we just hoped it didn't scare the you-know-what out of one of them!

The Cracker Tournament, though, wasn't just about fun. On August 13, 2004, Hurricane Charley, a Category 4 buzz saw with gusts hitting 150 mph, roared ashore and obliterated our marina docks. There was nothing left.

We were up and running by Labor Day, some three weeks later. But as the holiday weekend approached, Hurricane Frances—a gigantic, slow-moving storm with hurricane-force winds extending up to eighty miles from the eye and tropical storm-force winds reaching up to 300 miles from the center—was barreling toward the state's east coast.

We were under a mandatory evacuation notice because the islands were still a wreck, and we were expected to feel some effects because of the hurricane's large outer bands. Frances made landfall on September 5 just above Lake Okeechobee and took nearly two days to cross the state as it spun off twenty-three tornadoes.

Thankfully, we were spared the worst of it. The 2004 hurricane season was a wild one for Florida, with Charley, Frances, Ivan, and Jeanne striking the peninsula in a span of about six weeks.

Bent but not broken, we pushed back 'Tween Waters' opening to the weekend after Labor Day, which was the traditional weekend of the Cracker.

Of course, we didn't expect it would happen that year. But the legion of anglers who had faithfully fished the tournament had other ideas! Despite it all, they showed up, ready to wet their lines, and 'Tween Waters sprang back to life! We didn't have any docks, but everybody rolled with the punches.

Their help in getting us back on our feet when we had been knocked down touched me deeply. They energized us with a "Captiva Strong" resilience, and their "let's go!" spirit was just what we needed during those trying times.

This went way beyond simply business; this was a case of friends helping friends. I was so moved that the following year, I gave every participant a $100 gift certificate to the resort. While they couldn't use it that week, they could come back and enjoy it anytime they wanted.

They couldn't wait to use them! Only... not the next month or the next week. I'm talking about the next night, when I learned many of them used the certificates as poker chips. I got a kick out of that because it was such a fitting tribute to their adventurous spirits!

That sense of adventure must have rubbed off on me when some friends and I concocted a new way we could have even more fun and bring the community together in another type of large gathering. I'm not quite sure what got into us that day after a round of golf at South Seas Resort. We were in a celebratory mood because I had just opened a new addition to the restaurant now called the Sunset Room. I cracked a bottle of champagne with them as we relaxed.

So there we were, flutes in hand, bubbles dancing up to the rims. Maybe it was watching a tiny droplet of ice-cold water on the frosty neck of the bottle wiggle its way down through the condensation that set our thoughts meandering all the way to the idea of hosting a golf tournament. Voilà! The Champagne Open was born! The collective gasp of excitement could probably be heard all the way back on the first green at South Seas.

But then came the real challenge: how to spark people's imaginations with the invitations. We brainstormed a bit, each suggestion more elaborate than the last. "Let's send out a box with a cork in it!" someone suggested.

"Too subtle," I said. "It needs to really pop."

"How about an empty bottle of champagne?" another chimed in.

"Where's the pop in an already open bottle?" I wondered aloud.

And then a thought bubbled up: a full bottle of champagne! Talk about the promise of an actual pop! But it couldn't be just any bottle. This would be the Champagne Open's custom bottle, complete with a custom label in gold ink. Of course, with an eye toward keeping a lid on promotional costs, it was an affordable vintage. Besides, who wanted to risk shipping a bottle of Dom Perignon?

That settled it. We sent out 100 bottles, and we were on our way to the inaugural Champagne Open Golf Tournament.

We planned a crazy agenda; we wanted this to be a weekend to remember. We added canoe races, live music by the pool, and of course, so many bottles of champagne we needed an army of caddies to carry them all.

We drank enough bubbly to make the French proud! It was one of those weekends where the fun seemed to spill over into everything we did.

The Champagne Open became such a huge hit that before we knew it, we had to start reining in the invitation list; it grew too big and became the Champagne Invitational, an event where you had to know somebody to get an invite. But that only added to the specialness of what had started as a simple idea.

I still smile at how the tournament began—a crazy idea with friends after an afternoon on the links. Who knew that one spontaneous toast would

A custom-label bottle of bubbly gave our Champagne Open Golf Tournament real pop!

lead to something so unforgettable? I guess that's the magic of a good idea... and maybe a refreshing touch of bubbly.

Eleven

Waves of Loss, Currents of Change

I'VE WITNESSED THE SHIFTING temperament of the Gulf of Mexico for fifty years, from its calming waters lapping our shores one day to its stormy seas the next.

Similarly, amid the colorful and entertaining tales of my island life, there have also been moments shadowed by trial and uncertainty—times when the island's natural beauty was offset by the chaos of angry seas, and moments when I found myself grappling with the unsettling question of where my own life was headed.

I'll never forget one of the Gulf's menacing outbursts. Truth be told, I remember Thursday, October 22, 1987, like it was yesterday. And it's not because three days prior, the stock market had crashed in the then-largest one-day percentage drop in the history of the Dow Jones.

What came to be known as Wall Street's Black Monday was a historic collapse, but we islanders had an equally frightening issue to worry about—a historic collapse of our own.

I still have a copy of the *Fort Myers News-Press* coverage of the No Name Storm that threatened to swallow 'Tween Waters. Leading up to the danger, Captiva had weathered a series of Gulf storms that pummeled our shores.

It was as if the sea itself had become a giant claw, scraping away at the beach along Captiva Drive, slowly pulling the land into its grasp.

By Wednesday's moonless night, the sugar-white sand had been entirely consumed, replaced by the Gulf's unstoppable black water, which also washed away our beachfront tiki huts in a show of relentless force. The rising storm surge crept closer and closer to 'Tween Waters, jeopardizing everything we had been working for more than ten years to build.

But what we could actually *see* was only part of the peril. The thrashing water also ripped at the ground beneath Captiva Drive and undermined the pavement until it collapsed under its own weight and disappeared into the roiling Gulf.

Making matters even more fearsome, the moonless sky reduced the pitch-black night to near-zero visibility.

Shocked and concerned about the unfolding crisis, one of our residents, who was known as Duck Man, wanted to get a firsthand assessment of the situation and walked out toward the beach to check things out. He anticipated crossing Captiva Drive, but instead he stepped off the sheer edge of the nine-foot cliff that the road had become. He plummeted through the darkness until he hit the ground and broke his leg. It was devastating.

When the extent of the collapse became clear that morning, I called Mayor Porter Goss. I had seen a lot of things in my day, but never anything as threatening as witnessing for the first time the storm surge nearly at our doorstep. I'll be the first to admit I had to fight to keep my heart from pounding through my chest.

The mayor's wife, Mariel, answered the phone. "Mariel, it's Tony," I said. I could hear the breathless rasp in my voice. "We need to get Porter out here right away. We have a serious situation."

"What's going on? He's in the shower."

"You better tell him to make it a quick one." I tightened my grip on the phone. "We're in real trouble." It was only after we realized the water was beginning to recede that we were able to breathe easier.

Rebuilding Captiva Drive after 1987's No Name Storm swallowed the road and turned 'Tween Waters into an "alternate route" for cars moving north and south on the island.

With the road now unpassable, for the next week or so we allowed traffic to be rerouted via our property so food and supplies could continue to move on the island, and lines of cars slowly inched their way through 'Tween Waters.

Various work crews made things passable within a week, and then they built the road back with rocks. It was pretty amazing.

Afterward, there was some back-and-forth finger-pointing between the state and the county concerning infrastructure work and communication lapses that might have contributed to the collapse.

Regardless, the disastrous event led to a heightened community awareness of the efforts of the Captiva Erosion Prevention District, a taxpayer-funded initiative focused on managing and mitigating coastal erosion on Captiva.

In the distance is a massive pipeline that workers used after the storm to renourish the beach with offshore sand.

The collapse of Captiva Drive was a gut punch. But it was repaired, and life slowly returned to normal. The road's destruction, however, was a harbinger of the dismal unraveling of a lifelong relationship that had once seemed as stable as the shoreline but began to erode beneath me.

The Gulf waters could rise and fall with the tides, but this personal upheaval didn't simply pass—it reshaped everything. The uncertainty of the future loomed like a storm, pushing me toward a path I hadn't anticipated, but one from which that I couldn't turn away. One that shifted the very direction of my life.

I had known my business partner, Lloyd, as a boyhood family friend in Rochester and then a guiding mentor for more than half of my life. He was a great visionary who helped me get started in the hospitality business.

While he had many strengths, like all of us, he also had his flaws. Having all these years to ponder what happened between us, I think Lloyd got caught up in what I call the "founder's trap." His actions suggested that he thought he owned the entire company and could do whatever he wanted—but he was only a partial owner. Lloyd owned about thirty-two percent and I owned about twenty percent. And so together, with more than fifty percent ownership, we had the final say in the decisions regarding the company's direction, development, and operations.

After business was rolling and doing well, Lloyd did something I considered ethically questionable, and it began to really dig at me. All his life, Lloyd had loved to travel, which was fine. But he crossed a line with me when in the early 1990s he began writing travel articles for the *Captiva Chronicle* newspaper and charging his travel expenses back to our company, Rochester Resorts. His agreement with the publication was strictly personal, and it had absolutely nothing to do with our business.

I had my hands full running our Captiva operations while he was off on this new course, traveling more and more, and I raised my concerns with him a number of times about how he was funding his travels with our company's money. I told him I thought it was improper, but he continued, undeterred.

The situation weighed on me, but I couldn't immediately confront it head-on because I didn't want it to hinder my role in leading our growth. I was working ten- and twelve-hour days, not only on behalf of myself, but our guests, employees, and shareholders as well—including Lloyd.

Another issue that grew to concern me, because it had a direct impact on the quality of our operation, was Lloyd's hiring of friends or the family members of friends, regardless of their qualifications. This led to incompetent people in positions that had no real dedication and no experience in the business. But they were Lloyd's appointees, and some carried themselves as if they had a certain layer of protection from being held accountable for their job performance.

I couldn't allow that to stand. When I fired one of his appointees for poor performance, and then I found out later that Lloyd had made this person a manager at one of our other properties, that was the straw that broke the camel's back—I had spoken with Lloyd about the impact of his decisions on our business, but he dismissed my concerns.

When things came to this ethical crossroads, I walked the beach with Angie as the sun set on another long day. I remember turning to her, as clear as if it had happened yesterday, and I said, "If I stay, nothing's ever going to change. The only way things will be different is if I leave."

Those were some of the hardest words I had ever uttered. I knew my leaving would send a ripple through the board—and I hoped it would also send a message. I truly loved my work and our staff. I respected and appreciated our board members. And I especially cherished the longtime guests who had become like a second family. But I couldn't be a part of a company culture of Lloyd's making that, in conflict with my values, gave unethical behavior a pass.

But I knew deep down that if I wanted to see any real change in our leadership culture, I had to step away. Angie and I talked about it a lot. We weighed the pros and cons. In the end, she agreed with me, even though it was a tough pill to swallow. At the age of forty-three, the prime of my professional life, I left the company with a month's notice and quietly resigned from the board.

I made it a point to never go out and crusade against Lloyd to try to drive him out or anything. I figured time would fix things. While I was gone, Jeff Shuff, who was food and beverage manager, was promoted to general manager. Jeff did a fine job, but he didn't have the company shares I had, so he had to basically go along with whatever Lloyd wanted to do. That's totally understandable.

Lloyd's hiring of staff simply because they were friends or the family of friends created problems. Employing friends and relatives is fraught with hard-learned lessons; it's an extremely slippery slope. You must be mindful of their skills and abilities, while also ensuring there's a way to hold them accountable.

Discipline can be troublesome, and how you do that—particularly disciplining an employee for improper behavior—makes a world of difference, especially if they're a high-performing employee and you want to keep them.

Some employees Lloyd had hired acted as if they were entitled to special privileges because they had a real or perceived relationship with him. But I have never played favorites. If someone works for me, I hold them accountable, regardless of who they are. At least I do my best to follow that principle.

In the hospitality business, as in many other businesses, being on time for work is crucial. Not only does it contribute to the smooth operation of guest services, but there are also fellow staff members counting on the timely arrival of their co-workers to take over duties at the end of a shift so they can return to their personal lives and their families.

Our policy was that arriving late for work without a legitimate reason was grounds for termination. That was the clear expectation. If someone came in late without a proper excuse, I fired them.

An episode that has stuck with me through the years is hearing about one of the shareholders mentioning to another shareholder that, "That damn Tony fired my son." And learning that the other shareholder replied, "He fired mine, too." So, all of our employees, whether or not they were shareholders' family members or friends, were held to the same standards. I still have that same approach today.

Even my own nephew, Charlie, who once worked with us and lived in employee housing, was held to the same expectations.

My introductory speech to him went something like this: "I don't want to know any of the gossip floating around employee housing, unless somebody dies. And never be late for work, or I'll fire you. If you can't live up to the performance standards all your fellow employees are expected to meet, you'll be given the worst hours and the worst jobs until you improve. How does that sound?"

I'm thankful he took it to heart and worked to the same high standards as everyone else. Because that's another issue if executive leadership or managers hire family and friends—other employees watch and pay attention to see if everyone is treated equally. For Charlie, by the time he left, he had made friends with everyone because they knew there was no favoritism in his hire.

Another challenge I've had to navigate is how to discipline employees who outright buck the operational norms and values of the company. We used to have an all-hands-on-deck employee meeting once a year. We would all take time out from our jobs to gather as a team, and it was important to me that everybody attend; of course, if they came to me with a valid reason they couldn't make it, I would excuse them.

Well, one of our excellent bartenders, a guy who went by the nickname of Cowboy, was making great money because the Crow's Nest was hopping; in fact, all the bartenders and waitstaff were doing very well. Cowboy made it known ahead of our annual meeting that he wasn't going to attend—for no reason at all, other than he apparently didn't feel like it. Sure enough, when we had the meeting, he wasn't there.

That left me with the question of how do I hold him accountable? He was a great bartender, everyone liked him, and I didn't want to lose him. But I couldn't just let him slide. What kind of message would that send?

So, I called him into my office for a sit-down meeting. I don't know whether HR would approve of my solution to the problem these days, but I said, "Look, Cowboy, I like you. I think you're doing a great job. However, I think you made a big mistake not showing up for the meeting. But we can fix it."

Cowboy shifted uneasily in his chair as I continued. "Here's what I propose: during Christmas week, you can wash dishes for the entire week on the night shift, and I'll pay you our dishwashers' hourly wage, but there will be no tips. You can either choose to accept that condition, you can resign, or I'll let you go."

Where's Cowboy? Nowhere to be found in this shot from one of our must-attend annual meetings. His pre-declared, defiant "no-show" required a response to hold the popular bartender accountable.

So he took it and worked the full week. He got the message, and we settled things. The upside for him was he learned and understood the kitchen operations much better, and he was able to appreciate the vital work the dishwashers did. He continued to work for me for another couple of years before moving on to his next hospitality rodeo.

So sometimes you get lucky and employees come around to see the "why" in decision-making when it comes to personal accountability; sometimes you don't get so lucky and they go on their way.

Grappling with questions of personal responsibility and ethics, whether it concerned employees or Lloyd's problematic actions, was part of my growth and development as a leader. It can be tough to draw a line in the sand with those close to you.

Looking back, I realize just how much of a defining moment this breaking point with Lloyd was for me. It drove my decision to leave the management and the board of a company I had spent the better part of a decade building.

As the general manager, I was the one who took on most of the work. Day in and day out, I was on the job, the one people turned to whenever they needed answers. I was the one who knew the ins and outs, the nooks and crannies of the business. I was always there to keep things moving forward and growing our opportunity.

On the other hand, it was different for Lloyd. He had other business and personal interests and would come and go with the seasons, showing up more often in the winter months to escape the northern winters. He dipped in and out, while I was always on-site, grinding away to keep the place running.

But I had reached a personal fork in the road. Faced with either accepting what I saw as a troublesome corporate status quo or letting my actions speak for where I stood, maybe I chose the road less taken. It cost me some friendships. It cost me lost time, leaving behind what I loved. Not knowing what the future held was a leap of faith.

It was a difficult time. But as the years passed, I'm grateful Lloyd and I were able to patch things up. In the end, there was too much history between us to simply turn our backs on each other. We had been a big part of each other's lives for a long time. We occasionally got together to talk things through. I think he eventually understood where I was coming from, and I sensed that maybe, just maybe, he came to realize I was right after all.

Twelve

New Directions, New Adventures

AFTER STEPPING AWAY FROM the company, I found that life had a few adventures tucked up its sleeve. It was time to pivot in a new direction, so I earned my real estate license and joined the board of directors of the Sanibel Community Association (SCA), which today is known as The Community House.

I also worked with Fred McConnell, who was promoting Lee County as a tourist destination through his work on the county's Tourist Development Board, the forerunner of the current Tourist Development Council. In the mid-1980s, he launched his own venture, Florida Travel Marketing, Inc.

Fred invited me to accompany him on various working trips, and those experiences were a source of inspiration and growth. Every time we traveled to showcase what makes our area so special, Fred's wealth of experience gave him the ability to see the bigger picture. Watching him work was like a masterclass in hospitality and tourism marketing.

Under his mentorship, I picked up on the importance of storytelling—how every place has its own narrative and how the key to attracting visitors isn't just in splashy brochures (imagine, no internet!), but in how to help folks feel connected to a destination before they even arrived.

In many ways, I was learning to understand the hospitality business at a deeper level and with a much broader perspective. I would go on to work a stint at the Lee County Visitor & Convention Bureau. It was an honor to be selected to be involved there, and it would lead me to join the board of VISIT FLORIDA, the state's tourism marketing arm that works closely with statewide tourism development partners.

I eventually served as VISIT FLORIDA's board chair. To be honest, that still feels like an almost unbelievable accomplishment, because it was something far beyond anything I could have dared to imagine for myself.

It was one of those moments where I had to take a step back and think, "Wow, how did I end up here?" I was so grateful for the opportunity—although at first, I was definitely out of my comfort zone because there were representatives from the major tourism operations throughout the state.

But no matter how large their companies were, the professionals I served with were very welcoming and made me feel comfortable with who I was and the type of knowledge and experience I brought to the table.

A fun side story: Fred and his wife, Terry Abbey, would eventually join my team. Fred manned the front desk of 'Tween

Waters and Terry ran Beachview Cottages and Castaways Beach & Bay Cottages. They really had a knack for making people feel welcome and had the ability to roll with the punches that invariably arise when you're running a beach inn.

I chuckle when I think about one such episode with Fred at 'Tween Waters. It was the height of season, a time when some of our recurring winter guests might settle in for a month or more. In fact, their arrivals were often like reunions among old friends, and it wasn't unusual for them to make special requests during these extended stays.

Mr. and Mrs. Jones, longtime northern visitors, routinely requested two twin beds instead of a queen-size bed in their room. But the day was especially hectic, and we hadn't had a chance to switch out the beds by the time they arrived. As Mr. Jones approached the front desk, Fred, calm as you like, greeted him with his usual warmth.

Mr. Jones, about to spend the winter months in Captiva's sun-splashed warmth, was in a jovial mood and smiled at Fred. "Hey, Fred! How's it going?"

Shaking Mr. Jones' hand, Fred, ever diplomatic, took a breath and leaned in just slightly, as if sharing a secret. "We've got a slight situation, and I'm gonna need your help."

Mr. Jones nodded. "Sure. What do you need?"

"Well," Fred replied with a twinkle in his eye, "the team hasn't gotten around to bringing in the twin beds, so... would you mind sleeping with your wife tonight?"

Mr. Jones chuckled. "No problem."

The next day, when the team arrived to switch their bed to the twins, Mr. Jones waved them off with a grin. "You know, I think we'll stick with the queen for the rest of our stay."

And that is how you turn a potentially sticky situation into a charming little victory—with maybe a touch of unexpected romance to boot!

Meanwhile, a truly gratifying and unexpected turn came while I was serving on the SCA board. Things were humming along until a bit of a brouhaha erupted with the island merchants. The gist of it? The association was putting on fundraising gatherings of arts and crafts fairs and antique shows, and the local shop owners felt that people were more inclined to spend their money at our gatherings rather than in their stores.

Naturally, we had to come up with a plan—something to still serve as a fundraiser for SCA without stepping on the merchants' toes. So, the board got together to brainstorm.

I remember the wheels in my head starting to turn, and before I knew it, an idea hit me like a golf ball driven off a tee. "How about a miniature golf course? Over the Christmas holidays, no less!"

I figured we could get area businesses to sponsor a hole for a hundred bucks each, which would cover the costs (my labor was cheap!), and we could throw a fun community event that wouldn't hurt the local economy. Oh, and I promised we could pull it off on a shoestring budget.

I sketched the entire miniature course on a scrap of paper in about fifteen minutes—a windmill obstacle, a water hole, sand traps, the whole nine yards—or should I say eighteen holes? Before I knew it, we had a full-size miniature putt-putt course, and it was an absolute hit! On opening day, none other than Pat Flynn, the head golf pro at The Dunes Golf & Tennis Club, showed up with his caddie in tow and a full set of clubs in hand! The sight of him sizing up our little course like it was a PGA championship event elicited unforgettable smiles and laughter!

The design idea might've come quickly, but I didn't create the course alone; I had a fantastic group of islanders on the mini-links team. Folks like Ann Arnoff, Gordon Schopfer, and Roy Silvers were absolute troopers, helping me turn my doodle into reality.

We were able to build the foundation of the course thanks to Joe Mazzola, a longtime friend who kindly loaned us a stack of 4x4s from the lumber company. I stress he *loaned* them to us, because if we had kept them year-round for what we envisioned as an annual holiday event, they would've warped and been useless the following year.

Every year, after the event, we'd take the whole thing down, return the 4x4s, and rinse and repeat the next Christmas. Talk about a labor of love! I'd spend anywhere from two to three full days constructing the course. But, thankfully, we had support from the local service clubs, who helped run the event for the four days and nights.

One great guy I could always count on was Dick Muench. Together, we kept the miniature golf venue running like clockwork for four straight days and nights, from ten a.m. to nine p.m. We teed-off the day after Christmas and ran until December 29, and some days we had as many as 300 people come through. Rain or shine, the show went on, and it was such a fun community event for all ages. Year after year, we managed to raise $10,000 to

$12,000 for the association. And we kept this tradition alive for twenty years.

I can't forget to mention Bob Walsh of R.S. Walsh Landscaping. I've known Bob ever since I arrived, and he generously lent our holiday putting course fantastic foliage that really dressed up the event. He and his crew hauled in and set up fifteen-foot palm trees and a variety of lush plantings that really captured the island's beauty.

Now, being honest, my holiday miniature golf idea didn't exactly result in a personal hole in one. You might say I landed in a rough with my wife, Angie, who wasn't exactly thrilled with me vanishing for days to cheer on throngs of putt-putters during the holiday season, and I can't say I blame her. But God love 'er, she pitched in and helped a lot, even if she wasn't entirely on board with my latest escapade.

Eventually, when the SCA building was remodeled without carpeting, it was my golden ticket to retire the event, and I was able to head to the proverbial nineteenth hole to share years of memories with my friends and colleagues who helped pull off this special event.

SCA's Sanibel Shell Festival was another favorite island event for which I served as chairman. The ongoing festival is a long-standing tradition held on the first weekend of March. Its beginnings trace back nearly ninety years, and it attracts people from all over the world. That was a lot of work, with plenty of volunteer help.

Thirteen

Roots and Remembrance

In 1992, when I was forty-five, members of the board of directors asked me to rejoin the company after my two-year hiatus. I agreed, returned to the board, and I also was named vice president, with Jeff Shuff remaining as general manager. This time, though, things were going to be different. Lloyd, who had previously disregarded my ethical concerns, realized where I stood; he recognized my values and, more importantly, understood that I wouldn't waver on them.

A primary condition upon which I returned was the board's agreeing that Lloyd would no longer be our corporate attorney and that I would select the law firm. I selected Humphrey-Knott in Fort Myers, known today as Knott-Ebelini-Hart. Back then, Mark Ebelini was a young lawyer assigned to me. During the past thirty-five years, we have become great friends, and he does a fantastic job for us.

Lloyd, now in his mid-sixties, had recently undergone quadruple bypass surgery. He was recovering well; but Lloyd being Lloyd, he blamed me for somehow contributing to his health situation, even though his family had a long history of heart disease.

Before long, he was back on his feet and as on-the-go as ever. He began traveling again and writing about his exploits for the *Captiva Chronicle*, but he wasn't charging his travel expenses back to our company, which was still under the banner of Rochester Resorts.

The company was doing well, and I gradually settled once more into the business I loved, returning to my roots and a more familiar routine. But that sense of normalcy wouldn't last.

Over the Memorial Day weekend in 1994, tragedy struck in the most unimaginable way. Jory Dahmer, a much-loved bartender who had welcomed so many visitors and islanders to countless memorable times at the Crow's Nest with his infectious smile and friendly ways, was senselessly taken from us. He was shot and killed in a random act of violence that punctured our sense of living in an idyllic, tiny-island beach town. For seven years, Jory had been part of our 'Tween Waters family—heck, part of the *island's* family.

I'll never forget first hearing the gut-wrenching news. To this day, I still struggle to process what happened. I had seen him just a day or two before he was murdered on a warm June night. Jory had been full of life and promise. In addition to kayaking, he was an avid sportsman, and he loved participating in all kinds of island sports, including playing softball at the Sanibel Recreation

Center. He even competed in our inaugural International Kayak Classic.

Well-known and well-loved on the island, he had just finished working a busy shift that night, like so many nights before, and decided to take a walk on a quiet stretch of Captiva beach with his girlfriend, Sarah Wood, who also worked for us. The weather was calm and humid, with a light Gulf breeze on a dark, moonless night along the tranquil shoreline.

But that tranquility was shattered by the bullet that ended Jory's life. That he would even cross paths with his murderer was a fluke, a case of being in the wrong place at the wrong time. A suicidal twenty-one-year-old employee of a nearby resort, who was later convicted of murder, reportedly wanted to see what it would be like to kill someone with the 9 mm Beretta handgun he had just bought.

And just like that, Jory was gone. We were thankful Sarah survived, but the news of Jory's death hammered us like a tidal wave. Captiva had always felt like a world apart, insulated from the kind of random, lethal violence that happened elsewhere. We were a small community, as we remain today, tightly knit and protective of one another. It didn't seem possible that something like this could happen here, on this little island that had always felt like a safe haven.

We held a memorial with a service on the beach and a reception at the Crow's Nest. Jory ran on the beach every day, so we all returned to the shore to watch the sunset in his honor. The island mourned, and so did our 'Tween Waters family.

Jory's memorial plaque where he would often play softball at the Sanibel Recreation Center.

Jory was always focused on moving forward, and we realized we had to do that, too. There was no other choice—we picked ourselves up and pressed forward, even though the weight of our grief felt almost unbearable at times. Later, the island communities honored our lost friend with a memorial plaque where he once played softball at the Sanibel Recreation Center. It reads: Jory L. Dahmer Field. A Friend to Many. 1994.

The days that followed our period of mourning turned into weeks, and the weeks turned into months, the passage of time doing its best to heal our wounds. Like the coming and going of the tides, the rhythm of life returned, and soon we were celebrating the renewal of a Christmas season with a great tradition: our Christmas tree lighting ceremony.

The occasion had become quite the event, and Lloyd was in his element, hosting the annual party like a seasoned party pro. I couldn't help but think back to my boyhood in Rochester, when he would host neighborhood parties in the shadows of Lake Ontario; even then, it had been about community good times.

During one special tree-lighting ceremony, everyone was in great holiday spirits (as always!), and we did the countdown, then threw the switch to light the outdoor tree as cheers rang out. It was a great time with fellow islanders and guests alike, but I couldn't help feeling there was room for a little more excitement.

And that's when the fireworks went off in my mind—that's it! Fireworks! I devised a plan and brought our general manager, Jeff Shuff, into the holiday plot: without telling Lloyd, we secretly booked Zambelli Fireworks—one of the largest pyrotechnics outfits in the world.

A crowd gathers for a festive 'Tween Waters tradition: the lighting of the Christmas tree.

When the night's ceremony came, Lloyd was the grand master of ceremonies. But Jeff and I were the grand masters of surprise! As the lights twinkled on the Christmas tree, Lloyd wrapped up his speech, thinking it was all over. But just then—*WHOOSH!*—the first rocket shot into the sky and sliced through the exhilarating winter air.

BOOM! The explosion lit the night in a massive starburst of color as music thundered through the speakers. The crowd of more than 500 erupted, their cheers rising to meet the seemingly endless *POP, BOOM, BANG* of fireworks above, the entire scene suddenly electrified with energy.

Lloyd, completely caught off guard, tracked me down amid the crackling celebration, grabbed me by the shirt, and half-seriously grumbled, "How much is this costing us?" We both couldn't help but laugh. He genuinely enjoyed the spectacle. It was such a hit, Christmas fireworks became a new tradition.

The fireworks at the Christmas tree lighting must have lit a spark in Lloyd, propelling his idea to host a Millennium Party with a spectacular fireworks display on New Year's Eve 1999. We went all out—big boom-booms, more food than you could imagine, and drinks everywhere. We hosted three different, simultaneous parties: a black-tie event in the Wakefield Room, a classic beach vibe at Old Captiva House, and a rowdy crew at the Crow's Nest.

(From left) Yours Truly, Bob, and Lloyd celebrate in the Wakefield Room on New Year's Eve in 1999.

At midnight, a barge out in the Gulf lit up the sky with a thirty-minute fireworks display, celebrating both the new century and the fact that the computer apocalypse Y2K hadn't marked the end of civilization as we knew it. (Remember that doomsday scenario?) It seemed like the entire island, tourists and locals alike, swarmed the beach as one, champagne in hand.

All eyes were on the skies during our Millennium Party fireworks extravaganza!

One of the best moments? The next day, we got a check for $1,000 from Betty Jensen. Back in 1977, Betty and her late husband, "Red" Jensen, who passed away in 1996, bought and transformed a bayside marina and a collection of old Florida-style cottages into a landmark vacation destination a shell's throw from 'Tween Waters. Betty wanted to thank us for such an unforgettable night to usher in the new century. Now that's what I call a tight community!

Preparing for revelers to gather on the beach to welcome the new century at our fireworks display on December 31, 1999.

Fourteen

Life's Tempests

As the Millenium Party in 2000 faded from memory, I was hit in January 2001 with the news that Lloyd had passed away at the age of seventy-five.

It was hard to reconcile that such a lifelong acquaintance was gone. He had been a vibrant, worldly guy I looked up to as a boy. Then he mentored me in my early days in hospitality while I was still in my twenties. He had seen me grow into a young man who carved out his own path and established his independence, all the way to the point where I took a stand with him over business ethics.

Through it all, we had come full circle, and I was grateful we were able to patch things up and arrive at a point of understanding and mutual respect. His passing left me with a sense that an era had ended.

Following his death, I was named president and CEO at the age of fifty-four. Having helped build the company from the ground up, the consensus among the board was that my appointment comprised a logical succession plan. We were set for the future.

But that future could never have predicted the unspeakable tragedy of the 9/11 terrorist attacks at the Twin Towers in New York, the Pentagon, and on Flight 93 that crashed into a Pennsylvania field when the passengers heroically prevented it from reaching its intended target.

Those were dark times in our country. Travel tourism shut down in the wake of that horrific event; but like America itself, we eventually regained our footing and pressed forward. In 2003, we completed renovating the historical cottages, something Lloyd had always wanted to do. We opened the ceilings and restored the units to their original beauty. I had to smile at how wonderfully they turned out, and I think he would have really liked them.

Trying times such as those brought on by 9/11 were brightened by the chance to meet unforgettable guests in the 2000s. I think fondly of Barry Braun from the East Coast, who would visit with his wife. A talented artist, Barry always left behind a sketch—sometimes of the cottages, sometimes just something whimsical—and those drawings always remind me of them.

The turning of life's calendar pages, of course, has a way of balancing such joyful memories with moments of hardship. Just as we had reveled in the warmth of that Irish celebration, we would soon find ourselves facing a different kind of force, one far less inviting.

On Friday, August 13, 2004, Hurricane Charley raked Captiva with winds roaring at 150 mph, making it a strong Category 4 storm; gusts were even higher, peaking at near 175 mph. I had never really given any credence to the old superstition about Friday the thirteenth being a day of bad luck; after Charley, I wasn't so sure...

The raging storm made landfall slightly north of us, on the tiny, largely uninhabited island of Cayo Costa. Charley's typical counter-clockwise rotation meant we were located on the side of the storm with the highest wind speeds; thankfully, the hurricane barreled through at about twenty-five mph, a fast pace that helped limit serious storm surge.

The storm blasted in like a buzz saw in the early afternoon, and daylight allowed those of us who stayed at 'Tween Waters to witness its fury firsthand.

The winds toppled trees like matchsticks, especially the island's towering Australian pines. One crushed cottage #106, which fronted Captiva Drive and was named in tribute to J.N. "Ding" Darling, a multiple Pulitzer Prize-winning political cartoonist and avid conservationist who often vacationed at 'Tween Waters.

Charley's strength was immense, yet so was the resilience of the dozen or so of us who rode out the storm on-site. Once the hurricane passed, we immediately began to clean up the wreckage. Despite the damage, we found ways to transform the challenges we faced into moments of determination. I grabbed a chain saw and cut away the tree that had pulverized the Ding Darling cottage. I kept a large chunk of it as a symbolic trophy of sorts, still on display in our lobby.

The hurricane's destruction shut us off from the outside world, and we lived on the island like the Swiss Family Robinson, with no electricity for seventeen days. Fortunately, we knew we had a generator to power the kitchen and other essential systems, so we were able to eat pretty well as we got to work reassembling the property and our lives.

The Hurricane Charley "trophy cut" that came down on the Ding Darling Cottage, on display in our lobby.

Bent but not broken, we cleaned out the pool, where everything imaginable had blown in, and we had enough chlorine to keep the water in good shape.

Our routine was breakfast between seven and eight. Then we worked until noon, when we'd break for lunch, after which we'd work until about two in the afternoon—the most brutally hot time of the day.

Then we hung out at the pool, dipping and cleaning, because there was no running water. I can't tell you how great it was to have the pool, where we refreshed ourselves, with daytime temperatures hovering in the upper eighties to low nineties, with high humidity to boot. That typical August weather, combined with the lack of basic utilities, made recovery efforts even more challenging for residents and crews working to restore infrastructure functionality on the island.

We found moments of levity and camaraderie forged by the closeness of our band of survivors. The first to reach us were emergency response officials, who confirmed we were all okay and advised us that the island was under martial law.

"And that means no consumption of alcohol," they instructed us.

I hoped they didn't see the impish smirk on my face when I thought, *yeah, right*. If there was ever time for a cool, stiff drink, we were in the thick of it.

After a day spent cleaning up, like clockwork, we gathered at the *air-conditioned* Crow's Nest for dinner. *And cocktails*—both of which never tasted so good! Among our hardy group was a young chef named Jason Miller, who happened to be dating our general manager's daughter. Needless to say, our dinners were fantastic. Later, we hired Jason as an executive chef.

Just for kicks, I suggested we arrange all the chairs around the pool to look like we were open. We all got a chuckle out of it, but it helped create the appearance of normalcy amid the chaos. Maybe it was for our own sense of sanity.

Later, in a bit of a friendly rivalry, I learned that the South Seas Resort owners were flying around in helicopters and wondered out loud how come our pool looked so good and theirs were all inky black.

Before the storm, I had rented a forty-foot bucket-lift machine to do some painting, and it turned out to be extremely valuable. We raised an antenna to boost our cell service, which allowed us to let people know we could get up and running as soon as they opened the island to contractors. It was amazing to go up for a bird's-eye view. There wasn't a leaf on a tree. The canopy had been stripped bare, and you could see forever.

We learned that when Mother Nature knocks you down, you need to get back up. One particular act of defiance came from Angie. Determined to find out what happened to our Sanibel home and afraid of what she would find, she hiked ten miles to check on its condition.

During her long, solitary walk under a scorching sun, she encountered an eerie, consuming silence and utter desolation. Trees were gone or sat cockeyed, stripped bare. No birds. None of the prevalent tiny lizards normally skittering about. No screeching cicadas or buzzing mosquitos. Gratefully, she found our house still standing.

The next blazing, steamy day after a ten-mile return hike, Angie confronted a heavily armed National Guard unit, local police, the fire chief, and a small army of other first responders. They were on high alert at the Blind Pass Bridge, the only overland way onto or off of Captiva. She knew some of those gathered.

They exchanged greetings and a brief tale or two about what had just happened—the kind you might share with others who had just endured the same natural disaster. But it was only a moment before the small talk took a back seat when she tried to continue on her way across the bridge.

"You have to halt, ma'am," one of the guardsman instructed her.

"Halt?"

"Yes, ma'am. Captiva is under martial law and you can't cross."

She shifted on her tired feet and mopped the sweat from her dirt-streaked face. "Oh, *really*?" she said, her voice edged with defiant disbelief.

If you've ever faced a massive natural disaster that had not only nearly destroyed your way of life but also your dreams, you can probably understand her frayed nerves and the steel rod that fortified her spine at that moment—that, and the fact that Angie has never been one to shy away from sharing her opinion.

"Where were you guys yesterday," she said, "when we could have really used you?" She fixed her determined glare on them, then focused on one of the local first responders who knew her. "I was at 'Tween Waters yesterday, and I'm going back today."

"Angie," he said with a wince, "I don't think that—"

"What're you gonna do, shoot me?"

She caught a few half grins among the local guys. For the rest of the armed contingent, this exhausted, sweat-drenched, try-and-stop-me woman who had humorously challenged them must have been quite a sight.

After they huddled for a moment to discuss the situation, they agreed to take her in their Jeep. She climbed in, then they drove her along the beach because Captiva Drive was impassible to vehicles, and they dropped her in front of 'Tween Waters. It seemed that when faced with daunting odds, a little spitfire determination paired with a dash of humor can sometimes open doors that appeared firmly bolted closed.

Things were chaotic everywhere in the days after Charley. Due to the severity of the damage, Sanibel and Captiva were off-limits for about a week to residents who had evacuated before the storm hit. Only emergency personnel and essential workers were allowed to cross the Sanibel Causeway.

I knew it would be a rough recovery, and we needed to jumpstart our revenue stream to meet our financial obligations. Emergency management had set up a command center near the base of the bridge on the Sanibel side, and after a couple of days, I made my way to a meeting there and listened to their report.

Tensions were high because of the widespread devastation. Much of Southwest Florida was without power due to downed lines, damaged infrastructure, and fallen trees.

Everyone's world was upside down at this point. I had learned that a sense of humor was important to get through the unpredictable craziness life can throw at you.

So, when they opened the meeting up for questions, I jokingly asked, "When can we open for visitors? I have my Beachview Cottages ready to go. All I need is power."

Within a few seconds, a field supervisor from Lee County Electric Cooperative (LCEC) worked his way to me through the gathered crowd and handed me a credit card. "I'll take every unit. You'll have power tomorrow."

The LCEC team needed a place to stay and meals to nourish themselves in the grueling days ahead. And that was the start of our post-Charley business.

The crew stayed at the Beachview for a week, then moved to Castaways for another week, and then stayed at 'Tween Waters, where we served breakfast, lunch, and dinner every day for between forty and sixty line workers and technicians who labored to restore electricity to the island.

LCEC did tremendous work. The logistics of power restoration on Captiva were complicated by the fact that access to the island was limited by massive debris and damaged roadways. In some cases, their teams were forced to use boats and helicopters to reach areas, and they also faced issues with clearing roads to get trucks and equipment onto the island. Their coordinated, dogged persistence was something to see.

Hurricane Charley taught us all valuable lessons in teamwork. Islanders banded together through a strong sense of community. We all pitched in to clean up and rebuild. At the heart of the rebound was resilience in the face of devastation, the strength of togetherness, and the importance of humor and camaraderie in tough times.

On a business note, I learned one other lesson all of us in hospitality would do well to remember: He who opens first, wins. The 'Tween Waters community rebuilt in Charley's aftermath, proving that even in the face of overwhelming loss, we stood strong together.

Some years later, the same resilient spirit would carry us through the profound grief of losing a beloved staff member, Steve Slocum, who passed from a heart condition. He was such a wonderful guy who always had a smile. With his big, friendly personality, he was the first person people met when they drove in. He had worked with us for more than a decade, and it was a terrible blow for our employees and guests.

A few days before Steve's memorial service, Angie and I walked the beach in the morning and talked through what we thought we would like to say at his celebration of life in the Wakefield Room. As we gathered to exchange reassuring hugs and quiet smiles, it felt as if his spirit was still with us.

Several people shared heartfelt remarks, and then Angie read ours. I couldn't do it. No way. I would have never made it through without breaking down.

She drew a breath and said, "I picked this up out in my mailbox today." Then she began reading:

Greetings from heaven...

Dear Angie and Tony,

Please share this letter with all my friends and family. I arrived last week, and it is pretty wonderful here. I have no pain other than I miss all of you. I'm working with Saint Pete, but enjoyed a beer with God on arrival. Saint Pete has got me working at the gate with him. Here, we don't use day passes. We have eternal passes... And not everyone can get one.

Gocha and Lee, you would find this an easy job... We have no checkouts, no luggage, no cars, and everyone is very pleasant. Even the boaters! The golf carts never lose a charge, and the umbrellas and chairs magically set up and put themselves away each day.

Every day is season here, and each Tuesday night we have a cocktail party... It's a meet and greet for all of our former 'Tween Waters Inn guests and employees... I feel right at home.

For all my buddies at 'Tween Waters Inn, please carry the torch for me. Be warm, friendly, and welcoming because that is what makes 'Tween Waters such a great place to stay and work.

Jeff Shuff, thank you for hiring me twelve years ago. I loved every minute working for you, Tony, and Doug. Jason and your team always did a great job as well. I'll miss the excitement of Halloween... They don't do it here! But I'll be watching how you guys do with the parking during the lighting ceremony.

Angie, make sure you have a good handle on all the slackers and their appearance; I am counting on you. Webb and Les, think of me when you have that beer... Enjoy this celebration. Do not be sad. I am now living and working another wonderful life in heaven.

Special thanks and love to my mom and family. All of you will be in my heart forever. I look forward to seeing all of you at some time in the future. I see some people coming, so I have to make sure they have the right pass!

Many hugs, kisses, and love... To each and every one of you... Stevie.

When Angie finished, you could hear a pin drop. No one spoke after that.

Fifteen

Building More Than Memories

IN THE LATE 1990S, we stood at a crossroads as we continued to build 'Tween Waters into a premier vacation destination where visitors could create unforgettable memories.

It became clear that the land containing employee housing was too valuable to overlook as a potential site for expanding guest accommodations. So we decided to tear it down to make way for the construction of the Mangrove Building, with ten one-bedroom suites and two three-bedroom, two-bath suites.

Completing this project marked a turning point, but our work was far from over, and we turned our attention to the next challenge: two deteriorating eight-plex buildings on the edge of the marina, leftovers from the inn's rough-hewn earlier era. Their Harvest Gold shag carpeting—something considered stylish decades prior—had long since become a gnarled hazard that camouflaged sandspurs and ambushed unsuspecting bare feet. Not exactly welcoming.

The rooms were darn near claustrophobic. You could practically check for a newspaper at the front doors without ever leaving the beds. And their thin walls made privacy an unattainable amenity. These buildings weren't just outdated—they felt like an entirely different world compared to what we aspired to create.

During this transformative period, before we could replace those relics with the Coconut Building, we had a visitor who left a lasting impression—though not for the reasons we might have hoped.

One day, during the height of season, and completely unannounced, John F. Kennedy, Jr. walked into our check-in area. Rooms were in high demand, and he asked if we had anything available.

Unfortunately, our front desk person didn't recognize him and put him in one of those… let's call them "less-than-stellar" units. As you might guess, John Jr.'s walk-in visit quickly turned into a walk-out. And I couldn't blame him.

Even now, I wince a little thinking about it. Tragically, a few years after he stopped in, he perished when the small plane he was piloting crashed into the Atlantic Ocean off Martha's Vineyard—a loss that added a bittersweet layer to the memory of that day.

Building on the success of the Mangrove units, we pressed ahead with our next major facilities undertaking. In 1997, we said goodbye to those leftover eight-plex buildings.

With new plans in hand, we moved forward with a much-needed change, clearing away those structures and four other rundown units.

Using their same combined footprint, we built the Coconut Building, with twenty one-bedroom suites, twelve of them overlooking the bay and the other eight facing the courtyard and the Gulf of Mexico.

Construction of the Coconut Building, overlooking the marina on the bayside, combined modern comforts with great views and timeless island charm.

The Coconut has become very popular with small families. The units offer two queen-sized beds in the bedroom, a pull-out sleeper sofa in the living room, a compact kitchen, and great views.

The rooms are a far cry from the cramped efficiencies we had replaced, and I was thrilled with the result. If only John Jr. could have seen what we couldn't yet offer when he visited us; I'd like to think he might have stayed a little longer.

Resolving that challenge cleared the way for us to tackle the next, equally ambitious task: the time-worn structures that once comprised the Captiva Beach Motel-Apartments. These boxy duplex buildings sat on a narrow strip of land that ran east to west at the southern end of the property.

'Tween Waters was established in 1931, but the vintage Captiva Beach Motel-Apartment buildings had a history all their own.

Once upon a time, a pioneering Captiva woman named Dorothy "Dottie" Wakefield had owned them, though I can't quite recall if the buildings were included when she sold the 'Tween Waters property to Scott Hamilton and Jay Freeburg, from whom Lloyd and I bought the resort in 1976.

But I do remember the buildings. Eight squat and sturdy structures made of concrete block, they were more functional than appealing.

Each housed two units: a double-bed studio and a twin-bed studio. They were simple, to say the least, and didn't exactly offer much in the way of charm. So we made the decision to start fresh, and the result was the Areca Building.

To build the Areca, we demolished six of the outdated Captiva Beach Motel-Apartment buildings and transformed what remained into something we could be proud of—a more modern structure housing twelve total units. Eight were standard guest rooms with pool views, while the other four were more expansive, two-bedroom, two-bath suites, complete with a living room and a full kitchen.

The construction was no small feat. I recall it vividly. The pile-driving machine—akin to a massive hammer with the precision of a surgeon and the brute force of a wrecking ball—was positioned right behind our main pool. And when I say right behind, I mean it was practically shaking hands with the pool deck.

I still marvel at the patience of our guests. Imagine trying to lounge by the pool, soaking in the Florida sun, with a rhythmic, earth-shaking *BOOM, BOOM, BOOM* reverberating in your ears like cannon blasts as the ground quakes beneath your chaise lounge. It's a wonder anyone stuck around at all. But somehow, they did.

We gave the remaining two original buildings a facelift to better match the cottage styles of which we'd grown so fond. These buildings, closer to Captiva Drive on the Gulf side, blended in nicely with the rest of 'Tween Waters.

When the dust finally settled, we were the proud owners of our current 137-unit complex. But we weren't done yet. The time came for reimagining the Spa and Fitness Center.

For years, the spa had been wedged in the bottom of the Areca Building, and the fitness center was located underneath the Mangrove Building. It was time for an upgrade.

Jeff Shuff, our GM, was in charge of the renovation—and what a project it turned out to be. Ironically, at a cost of $1.2 million, it was the same amount we had paid for the entire 'Tween Waters property back in 1976. Funny how things work out.

A young lady named Georgie ran the spa as an independent operator, and her spa treatments were stellar. Countless brides and their bridal parties, stressed-out guests, or anyone just needing a moment of peace and relaxation found solace there. Massage therapy. Body treatments. Facials. Manicures and pedicures. It was a little oasis, and Georgie made sure every guest left feeling pampered and rejuvenated.

By this time, things were humming along smoothly at 'Tween Waters, especially during the sweet spot of high season that stretched from mid-February to mid-April, when the resort truly came alive with the buzz of guests.

We had always prided ourselves on our food and beverage offerings. But as happens from time to time, you need to shake things up to keep your edge. So I came up with an idea that was equal parts daring and fun.

What if Angie and I, as special "guest chefs" for a night, created and cooked a custom menu of offerings? Angie said she was game, so she and I set up shop in the kitchen and put together our personal menu of seven unique dishes to go along with some of the restaurant's regular menu selections.

The night turned out to be a whirlwind. We served 164 guests, and 120 of them chose from our creations. It was a fast-paced, exhilarating experience, and the guests loved it. Angie was a trooper, but after that culinary high-wire act, even she said, "That's it. I'm one and done."

We found other ways to make the inn feel like a true home away from home. Tuesday nights became something special with our meet-and-greet parties by the pool. Each guest would get a name tag imprinted with their hometown, and before long, people were mingling and getting to know each other.

The next day, newfound friends were playing tennis, getting together over a game of cards, or partaking in whatever other interest they discovered they had in common.

Bob Calvert, one of our beloved longtime guests, became the ambassador of these gatherings, making everyone feel welcome. And he made sure that I, as the general manager, greeted each and every guest. It was heartwarming to see how these little moments turned former strangers into friends. Angie and I grew close with so many of these visitors who returned year after year.

One day, I suggested to Angie that we take it a step further—why not invite our long-term guests to our Sanibel home for a cocktail party? We sent out invitations, asking guests to remove their shoes as they entered our home with its Japanese-style décor and teak floors. About twenty-five couples joined us, everyone padding around in socks or barefoot. Angie, true to form, prepared delicious hors d'oeuvres while Dan Kinsley tended the bar. The evening had a special kind of magic to it.

Dan had done a wonderful job on the invitation logistics, keeping track of the RSVP list. But he was having a tough time getting a response from an elderly couple after asking them about it a number of times. Finally, we needed a headcount, so Dan made one last appeal.

"Will you be able to join us at Tony and Angie's for the cocktail party?"

The couple exchanged glances before responding. "Is he going to try to sell us something?"

I couldn't stop laughing when Dan told me that! Apparently, they thought it was one of those resort sales pitches disguised as a cocktail party, but it was purely about friendship.

At the end of the night, I got a kick out of seeing 100 shoes piled on our steps. I was struck by the notion of how each pair told a story—a little reminder of the lives that had mingled together for a few hours of conversation and laughter. It was such a simple thing, yet it brought me a satisfying grin. As the party came to a close and the last couple went to put on their shoes to leave, the husband realized the remaining pair of men's shoes weren't his; someone had taken his shoes by mistake!

Recreating the cocktail party shoes shenanigan at a recent family gathering. It was a shoo-in for a smile!

The next morning, at our regular buffet breakfast for everyone at 'Tween Waters, we set up a can't-miss display with the leftover men's shoes, complete with a sign: *Please help me find my rightful owner!* Folks got a good chuckle out of it—a fitting, lighthearted end to a truly memorable night.

These were the years during which, every December, we made sure to pause for an employee business meeting that allowed us to take a measure of the past year and kind of reset for the new year to come.

After the meeting, it became a tradition to host a company Christmas party. For the first hour, the Crow's Nest came alive with the laughter and camaraderie of our staff. Then Angie, with help from the staff, would prepare a beautiful buffet—cabbage rolls, stuffed mushrooms, antipasto skewers, Italian chicken, the works.

We had upward of 250 to 300 people because spouses and a few other folks also attended. After dinner in the Old Captiva House, people would go back to the Crow's Nest for more dancing and libations.

I can still picture the housekeeping staff and the grounds crew, who always dressed to impress for the occasion. But what lingers with me even more is the joy and camaraderie. The sense of togetherness that gave the night the mood of a genuine family celebration.

Eventually, things changed and we no longer held the Christmas party. Though we tried bringing in an outside caterer for a while, it was never quite the same. I really miss those times. The unforgettable smiles and laughter and the way the holiday spirit brought us all together still echoes with me today.

Sixteen

Heart of the Inn

OF COURSE, WHEN YOU have the pleasure of spending time with recurring guests who become fast friends, the smiles and laughter are never far behind. The Browns from Atlanta are among them.

They honeymooned at 'Tween Waters nearly forty years ago and continue to return to vacation. We have become great friends.

Going back decades, they have kindly introduced us to their friends who have also stayed with us. The Keoghans from Ireland, along with other guests, leap to mind.

Tony and Joan Keoghan have been coming to 'Tween Waters for more than twenty-five years. They were the parents of two small boys when they first arrived. Over time, the boys grew, and one of them, Connor, eventually decided to get married to a gal named Fiona. Angie and I were delighted to be invited to the wedding in Dublin—and yes, we attended the ceremony on the gorgeous Emerald Isle. What a time! It was early December, and we weren't quite prepared for the cold Irish winter, but the warmth of the Keoghans and their friends more than made up for it. We jokingly told their other son that if he ever got married, he should avoid the winter months. The family still visits to this day.

After years of growing friendships with families like the Keoghans, life presented a further opportunity for connection and growth.

It was around this same time, in 2007, that I was approached by a gentleman who introduced me to an organization called TEC, now known as Vistage. He pitched it as a group of local CEOs and business owners who gather once a month, along with a facilitator, to share ideas, tackle challenges, and offer guidance to one another. Kind of like a peer advisory group from non-competing business sectors.

At first, I wasn't exactly sold. In all honesty, my initial reaction was, "What could they possibly know about my business? I'm already the expert here." Looking back, I realize how arrogant that attitude was. I thought I had everything figured out. But I was wrong.

I agreed to give it a three-month trial—ninety days to see if it would be worthwhile. I couldn't have predicted that those ninety days would turn into fifteen years before I retired from the group in 2022. What started as skepticism evolved into one of the most enriching experiences of my professional life.

Dan Burnell was our facilitator and challenged us all the time. We met as a group for a full eight-hour day once a month. Then for two additional hours, Dan was available to meet personally in one-on-one sessions.

At the outset, I thought the membership was pricey, but it turned out it was priceless. It seemed everyone benefitted. I had an "aha!" moment when I realized that expertise isn't just about what you know. It's about what you're willing to learn. Sometimes, one of the smartest things you can do is admit that you don't know it all.

There's something that fosters a bond unlike any other when you're in a room full of people who truly understand what it means to carry the weight of a business, along with a personal life often impacted by those challenges. The group even helped me navigate a difficult time with Angie's health.

The return on investment, both in the group and in myself, was so much more than I had expected. Beyond the business benefits, the true value came from the personal growth I experienced. It's interesting how life can hand you vital lessons when you least expect them.

The experience proved crucial when it came time for me to tackle succession planning. The clarity and direction I gained from those discussions helped me set the company on a path for long-term success.

When I first started thinking about a succession plan for the company, I wasn't in any particular rush. I knew it was a decision that required time, patience, and, most importantly in my mind, someone with both an interest in the business and a connection to its history.

In the back of my mind, I hoped to find a person who not only shared the company's values but also understood its roots and the story behind it. After giving it some thought, the first person who came to mind was my nephew, Charlie.

Charlie was living with his wife and kids in Atlanta at the time, and I admired the way he had handled himself and his responsibilities when he'd previously worked for me as a rank-and-file team member and lived in employee housing. I thought he could be a great fit—someone I trusted who would feel a bond with what we had built from the ground up.

So I reached out to him. Although he said he was honored that I had considered him for such a significant role, he ultimately declined. He had done his due diligence, and I could tell it was a thoughtful decision on his part. We talked it over, and I respected that it was probably the best decision for him and his family.

After that, I let a few months pass, trusting that I would find the right person. And that's when Boots Babcock approached me on a completely different matter.

Boots and her husband, Kingman, had been original investors in a Sanibel property called the West Wind Inn, now known as the West Wind Island Resort. They were also original investors in Rochester Resorts.

Ironically, Kingman was a familiar face from my past—he was one of the bachelor crew who lived next door to my childhood home during summers in Rochester. Life has a funny way of circling back, doesn't it?

Over the years, the Babcock family, including their son, Doug, had vacationed at both 'Tween Waters and the West Wind Inn at a time when the West Wind wasn't yet a part of our Rochester Resorts portfolio. Doug grew up to have a background in finance and had spent years working on Wall Street before he decided to take his life in a different direction and moved his family to Connecticut.

Boots wondered if I might talk with Doug about possible investment opportunities in Fort Myers while he was down this way for a family reunion. I was more than happy to speak with him, so I invited Doug to coffee.

After chatting for a while, I realized there might be something beyond simply random investment opportunities. So I asked him directly, "Would you ever consider moving down here and becoming part of our succession plan?"

It was a big question, and I didn't expect an answer right away. He said he would like to explore the opportunity. So he and his wife, Paige, visited several times with their young kids as Doug did his due diligence for such a major decision.

Beyond the business opportunity, Doug and Paige wanted to get a good sense of what life here would be like, not just for Doug professionally, but for their whole family. It was a big move; it would mean selling their house in Connecticut and uprooting their lives.

After thinking it over and weighing all the variables, we all agreed it was a wonderful fit. Doug and his family took the leap, and he came on board.

We set up a three-year plan to get him started, and I have to give credit to my TEC/Vistage colleagues and Dan Burnell for helping me develop a solid understanding of how to implement a succession plan.

Of course, Doug needed to learn the ropes of the business. So that first year, I put him through the mill—budgeting, sewer school, housekeeping, food and beverage, maintenance. He got a taste of everything; having been through it all from the ground up myself, I knew this would fully ground him in the nuts and bolts of the company.

After a couple of years, Doug became an absolute wiz with our finances. It was around this time that Jeff Shuff, who had been such an integral part of the company, decided it was time to retire. That move opened the door for Doug to step into the role of vice president and general manager.

Doug was a "numbers" guy, no question. But what truly set him apart was his penchant for ideas—big ideas. And one of those that had been circling in his mind was the possibility of acquiring the West Wind Inn on Sanibel—the very place where he had spent countless boyhood vacations with his parents and siblings.

There was something poetic about it, and I could see why he was drawn to the thought of West Wind becoming part of our portfolio. The idea wasn't just intriguing—it was compelling. But excitement aside, I couldn't shake a certain personal anxiousness. This would be my first dive into the world of mergers and acquisitions. As exhilarating as that might sound, it was also unfamiliar territory. And I've learned that venturing down an unknown road in business can be filled with big potholes. That's why preparation was key.

Doug started working on the numbers, and we secured appraisals of the properties involved, along with doing all the other due diligence we needed to assess the merits of the possible acquisition.

Doug's mom, Boots, was already a shareholder at Rochester Resorts, which made things a bit more personal—and complicated. And, of course, other Rochester Resort shareholders would also have a stake in any potential deal. There was a boatload of moving pieces—so many things that could unravel. The kind of what-ifs that keep you up at night.

As things unfolded over several months, Doug and I were able to buy out a few of the other West Wind partners to strengthen our position. But the real challenge lay ahead: getting every shareholder on board. To make the deal work, we needed to change our bylaws, which required unanimous approval—100 percent "yea" votes.

I knew how tenuous that prospect was. A single holdout could have derailed everything. Deals like these are not just about numbers; they're about people. Their interests, doubts, goals, and agendas. I worried that some small but significant detail, or someone's uncertainty upon awakening the morning of the vote, could unravel the whole thing.

Aware that I was anxious about the vote at that afternoon's annual meeting, our attorney asked me if he should be present. I could feel the unease in my gut, but I told him no. I wanted to believe things would work out okay; I was certain our company books were strong and provided a solid foundation for shareholders to feel confident in our leadership.

Still, I knew better than to assume anything. The annual meeting kicked off at five p.m. By 5:05, the results were in. Every shareholder had voted "yes." I let out a breath I didn't realize I had been holding. We would acquire the West Wind Inn.

When I relayed the news of the 100 percent vote to our attorney the next day, he gave me a wry smile. "I'll mark that down as an exception."

I understood where he was coming from. Unanimous votes are rare in the world of business, and I knew how fortunate we were to get the deal done. But behind the relief, there was also a deeper sense that preparation had carried us through.

Acquiring the West Wind Inn prompted us to rebrand from Rochester Resorts to Sanibel Captiva Beach Resorts, a name we felt better captured both our mission and the essence of our portfolio. Doug, as president and CEO, is in charge of the day-to-day operations.

What had started as a casual conversation over coffee some fifteen years ago has become successive and successful chapters in the ongoing story of our company. I'm reminded that while we can plan and strategize, sometimes the best decisions are the ones that unfold naturally over time, with a little faith and a lot of trust in the quality people with which we surround ourselves.

Seventeen

Hardship and Heritage

Things were popping in 2009 with my board membership at VISIT FLORIDA, the official tourism marketing entity for the state, and my involvement broadened my professional perspective and knowledge.

When I think back on the period I worked with the organization, I can't help but feel appreciative of the people who supported me throughout my time there.

I must mention my fellow board members at the time: Walter Banks, owner of Lago Mar Beach Resort and Club in Fort Lauderdale and Russ Kimball, general manager of the Sheraton Sand Key Resort on Clearwater Beach.

Both Walter and Russ, one of VISIT FLORIDA's founding board members, have a deep well of knowledge and experience in our field and had a way of making me feel welcomed. Their insights and advice were invaluable as I found my footing in this larger business arena.

I also had the pleasure of meeting Ed Fouche, who joined the board at the same time I did in around 2006. Ed was a senior vice president at Disney, and he understood international travel on a whole other level. Ed and I rose through the ranks of VISIT FLORIDA together, and he eventually became the chair, with me set to take over the following year.

But things didn't go as planned. VISIT FLORIDA was hitting some headwinds that involved state funding. Board members asked if I'd be willing to wait one more year before stepping into the chairmanship. The idea for Ed staying in the position for another year was that he, and Disney's political influence, could help smooth out the funding issues in Tallahassee.

VISIT FLORIDA receives part of its funding from the state, which means it often has to navigate political considerations. That's why having major industry veterans like Ed involved with the board can help bolster the organization's ability to keep the state focused on investment in the tourism industry, which is a massive part of Florida's economy.

I didn't have a problem delaying my chair position for a year; I wasn't building a resume or looking to climb any kind of corporate ladder where I was pressing to get that feather in my cap.

For Ed, unfortunately, extending his service as chair couldn't have come at a worse time. A bolt-from-the-blue disaster erupted in a way that threw the state tourism industry into a dreadful state of chaos.

On April 20, 2010, a catastrophic explosion occurred at an offshore oil well in the Gulf of Mexico some forty miles off the coast of Louisiana. The Deepwater Horizon oil spill was one of the largest environmental disasters in U.S. history. The explosion killed eleven workers and released about 134 million gallons of crude oil into the Gulf.

Thankfully, Sanibel and Captiva didn't experience the calamity of oil washing ashore, as did areas of the Panhandle and parts of Louisiana, Mississippi, and Alabama. But we were far from untouched by the disaster.

The event caused widespread concern among potential tourists about the condition of all Florida's Gulf beaches. This perception created a significant challenge for us because it generated uncertainty among potential visitors. This led to cancellations and a decline in bookings during what is typically one of the most important seasons for Florida's tourism industry—spring break and summer vacations.

Of course, the drop in bookings also had a ripple effect that impacted local restaurants, shops, tour operators, fishing guides, and local attractions that depend on a steady flow of tourists.

During this chaotic period, I sympathized with Ed, who was caught in the thick of it. The responsibility of responding to the situation as the chair of VISIT FLORIDA landed on his shoulders.

I couldn't help but admire the way he remained calm and focused as he muscled through it. Under his leadership, the organization worked tirelessly to restore Florida's image as a safe and beautiful place to visit, reassuring potential travelers and boosting recovery efforts for businesses reliant on tourism.

Even though our beaches remained pristine, misplaced public fear was a powerful deterrent. It's so interesting how people sometimes forget that bad news spreads faster than good news, and even though our beaches remained gorgeous, just the anxiety over possible oil contamination was enough to slow down bookings.

If that weren't bad enough, we were still grappling with the lingering effects of the 2008 global financial crisis, a years-long economic recession triggered by the collapse of the U.S. housing market. The event spurred declines in leisure and business travel as households and corporations tightened budgets. Even after the economy began improving in 2009, cautious consumer spending and a slow return of business travel meant a prolonged recovery period.

The one-two punch of fearful public perception surrounding the Gulf Horizon oil spill and the economic collapse fueled a sharp drop in occupancy rates. What's known as our ADR (Average Daily Rate), the bread and butter of how innkeepers measure performance, took an enormous hit. The entire industry seemed to be getting hammered.

But amid all that turbulence, a new opportunity appeared in the form of advice from two trusted colleagues. Both Russ and Walter, seasoned voices in the industry, told me about the Southern Innkeepers Association. "You've got to join," they said.

And honestly, I'm glad I did. It's been one of the best professional decisions I've ever made. I'm still a member over a decade later. We meet annually, traveling to different areas, both in Florida and out of state. These discovery junkets are fantastic as a mix of education and camaraderie. The social aspect is super, but what really sticks with me are the speakers we get.

Recently, for example, we hosted Horst Schulze, a hospitality industry legend who helped launch the Ritz-Carlton in the early 1980s. He helped to define the company's legendary customer service philosophy, which emphasizes personalized, exceptional experiences for guests.

And here he was, now eighty-five years old, speaking to our group for almost an hour, and he didn't need a single note. That kind of presence, that kind of well-earned wisdom, is something you don't soon forget.

Horst began his career as a fourteen-year-old busboy in a German hotel and eventually worked his way up through various positions in Europe's finest hotels.

I felt a certain kinship with his "work your way up" journey, as I had shared a similar path. My first steps in hospitality weren't in a luxurious hotel, but in concrete-caked boots helping to build the community pool at the Nutmeg Condominiums on Sanibel a lifetime ago. Those early days laid the foundation for a career built on dedication and always striving to do top-quality work and deliver superior service for our guests.

This mentality of persistence has followed me throughout my professional life, including one of my proudest achievements: securing 'Tween Waters Inn a place on the National Register of Historic Places in 2011, a designation made possible with the help of colleagues on the VISIT FLORIDA board, for which I am forever grateful.

I can't tell you how many people have posed for a picture with that marker over the years—I wish I had a nickel for every time I see someone stop to snap a photo with it. It's a reminder of how far we've come and the history we've preserved.

As a steward of this special place, I'm both thrilled and humbled to have garnered for our property and the people who comprise its heartbeat such a prestigious designation. It recognizes the resort's rich historical significance and contribution to the region's cultural heritage. The acknowledgement not only honors 'Tween Waters' storied past but also ensures its protection for future generations, solidifying its legacy as a Florida landmark.

A plaque denoting the designation is near the entrance, close to the historic Old Captiva House restaurant. It reads: 'Tween Waters Inn was established on Captiva Island by F. Bowman and Grace B. Price in 1931. They started the inn with a single building and expanded it over the next thirty years, adding guest cottages, a marina, and other buildings as they built their remote tourist destination into a favorite winter resort for wealthy northerners.

Bowman and Price provided guided fishing trips for guests, and Grace offered entertainment and dining in the inn's Old Captiva House. 'Tween Waters' early visitors included Anne Morrow Lindbergh, wife of famed aviator Charles Lindbergh. Although she never stayed at the inn, she drew inspiration from Captiva for her best-selling book, *Gift from the Sea* (1955).

Another renowned visitor was J.N. "Ding" Darling, a conservationist and renowned editorial cartoonist who won Pulitzer Prizes in 1924 and 1943. Darling wrote and drew while staying at 'Tween Waters Inn for seven winter seasons between 1935-36 and 1941-42. He also helped establish the Sanibel National Wildlife Refuge, named in his honor in 1967.

The same year the inn was listed on the National Register of Historic Places, I found myself standing on a stage I hadn't quite expected, inducted as a laureate into the Junior Achievement Hall of Fame.

To say I was surprised would be an understatement. I was so humbled and honored. The hall of fame selection honors folks deemed to have made significant contributions to their industries and communities, often serving as role models for young people, in alignment with the organization's values of empowering future generations.

The ceremony at the Coconut Point Hyatt in Estero was quite an affair. The grand ballroom was filled with 600 or 700 people, all dressed for the occasion, and there was so much positive energy in the air. Two of us were honored that night, and my speech was the second one on the program. I still remember how it felt getting ready to step up to the podium. It was kind of neat, honestly, in that way where your nerves mix with a quiet focus.

I had practiced my speech meticulously—memorized it, in fact. I didn't want to rely on notes. I wanted to let my preparation guide me, but I wanted to speak from the heart. And when the time came, I managed to speak for a solid ten or twelve minutes with no notes. That might sound like a small detail, but in that moment, it felt like a personal triumph, and I was proud to have achieved it.

What made the evening even more special was the presence of so many friends who had come to celebrate with me and share the moment. The organizers sent me a video of the event afterward, and I still have it. It's one of those memories that sticks with you, not just for the accolade, but for the feeling of it all—the people, the mission of uplifting young people, and the quiet sense of accomplishment. Pretty cool, really. It's a moment I'll always cherish.

Looking back on this period, it wasn't always the easiest of times, but it was filled with lessons, the forming of personal friendships through professional growth, and milestones that I wouldn't trade for anything.

Eighteen

Creativity, Crisis and Comebacks

Persevering through the challenges in the wake of Gulf Horizon the oil spill, our occupancy rates rebounded and we were in an improved financial position. With more resources to reinvest at 'Tween Waters, we were eager to focus on projects that would enhance our guests' experience. One of our first undertakings was installing a geothermal system for the pool.

The system works by tapping into the earth's natural stable temperatures below the surface. So, in the winter, the mechanism draws heat from the ground to warm the pool. During the hot summer months, it reverses the process, pulling heat out of the pool and dissipating it into the cooler ground, effectively cooling the water.

It was an innovative solution that allowed us to heat the pool during chilly winters without relying on propane. Just as importantly, we could cool the pool during the scorching summers. Now, no matter the season, the pool stays a comfortable eighty-four degrees year-round.

I'll never forget the first time our summer guests jumped into the pool, expecting the typical hot-bath water, only to be greeted by that refreshing temperature. The surprise and delight on their faces were priceless, and I knew we had an additional edge over our competitors. It was one of those seemingly small but ultimately meaningful victories that felt like a reward for thinking ahead and investing in something that would make a real difference.

Not long after, a further idea sparked my interest. I couldn't ignore how the tangled web of electrical power lines running along Captiva Drive cut across the horizon and scarred our otherwise stunning, unobstructed views of the shimmering Gulf of Mexico. They stood out like dark, jagged lines that marred the serene backdrop we all cherish. The situation dug at me because those ugly wires ruined the beautiful views we wanted our guests to enjoy.

So I approached the board with a proposal. I asked for their approval to explore the cost of burying those utility lines, knowing it would be a significant investment. They agreed, and we spent about $15,000 on just the engineering study to see what it would take. We could apply that cost toward the final project if we proceeded, and after some consideration, the board gave me the green light.

In the end, we invested about $250,000 to put those lines underground. While I was clear with the board that this wouldn't necessarily improve profits, I felt strongly that the improvement in the property's appearance was worth every penny. Once completed, the difference was amazing. The unobstructed view allowed guests to take in the full beauty of the Gulf, unspoiled by a rat's nest of wires cutting across the horizon.

One of the more practical benefits of having underground power lines is simple common sense: they're better protected from high winds, flying debris, and falling trees, which can take down above-ground lines during powerful storms. On top of that, below-ground lines allow utility companies to restore power faster after severe weather. It's one less part of the grid they have to worry about fixing after a hurricane.

Of course, there's always someone with a different perspective. One guest approached me to say they missed seeing the birds that used to perch on the lines.

It just goes to show you that no matter how much effort you put into making improvements, you can't please everyone. But overall, I think we made the right call, and it's those kinds of decisions that have shaped the character and charm of 'Tween Waters.

With the power lines buried and the geothermal system working wonders, things were humming along. But we didn't rest on our laurels. During our peak months, the pool area could get crowded, especially with families and naturally rambunctious kids making the most of their vacation fun.

That's when Doug proposed a solution that extended our outdoor offerings with additional elbow room and a more relaxing alternative. He suggested eliminating one of our tennis courts to build a second pool, which we named the Serenity Pool.

It was a smart move, given how busy the main pool—now affectionately known as the Play Pool—could get, especially when kids were diving in and playing boisterous games of Marco Polo. The Serenity Pool, as the name suggests, has become a peaceful oasis for those seeking a place to unwind. While it's a favorite of many of our adult visitors, kids are always welcome too, as long as they keep things calm.

What made this even more satisfying was that we could adapt our geothermal infrastructure to the new pool as well. We were thrilled to have the Serenity Pool, the Play Pool, and our two Jacuzzis heated and cooled using the efficient, environmentally friendly geothermal strategy.

With such a splashing success behind us, it seemed we were in a mode to refine and reimagine what 'Tween Waters could be. Each project brought us closer to our vision of a resort devoted to delivering an elevated guest experience.

But there was one major renovation I had been putting off for years: the kitchen. When we bought the property back in 1976, the kitchen was already forty years old, and although I had done some remodeling over the years, it had never been a complete overhaul. I kept hesitating, wondering how we could pull off such a massive renovation without disrupting our guests.

During our minor remodels, when I would picture such a colossal transformation, I felt like joking with our breakfast guests, "Would you like a side of sawdust with your eggs?" But I realized I couldn't keep managing our kitchen problems as they popped up—I needed to step back and address the overall needs of our dining operation.

Of course, a project like that came with a mountain of questions. How much would it cost? How long would it take? And the biggest question of all: how could we continue to serve our guests when the kitchen was out of commission?

At one point, we thought we were ready to start the project, but permitting turned out to be a nightmare when it came to getting approvals for a temporary commercial kitchen, which we needed to bridge the gap between tearing out the old facility and getting the new one up and running. No one with whom we initially spoke seemed to know much about it or how to build one.

Constructing a temporary commercial kitchen requires the kind of planning that makes a Rubik's Cube look like child's play. Not only do you have to meet health and safety standards, but it has to function efficiently. It's not the kind of job where you can just throw together a few appliances. I mean, talk about electrical demand. Our kitchens run high-powered commercial appliances that demand significant power capacity.

Then there's proper ventilation, water supply, waste disposal, food storage, and the actual cooking equipment—all of which must meet strict regulations. It takes expertise in both kitchen operations and logistics to ensure the temporary space is fully functional and compliant with local codes.

It was a monumental proposition that left us scratching our heads, and we had to speculate on the costs ourselves. We estimated the total renovation would run between $2 million and $3 million, which also included a full overhaul of the Old Captiva House restaurant.

We got ourselves on the right track when we sought companies that specialized in setting up temporary kitchens during major renovations like ours. It wasn't cheap—about $15,000 a month, to the best of my recollection—but when they got it up and running, it was impressive. A complete kitchen with everything we needed—including air-conditioning.

The interim facility had to ensure that the electrical system could handle the power load safely and reliably. I owe a big tip of the hat to Robert Greco at ACRA Electric, who was indispensable. Not only did he lead a customized electrical service installation just so we could even *start* demolition, but he also powered up the new temporary kitchen, the Crow's Nest, and three massive semi-trailers parked on-site for refrigeration. It was a logistical maze, but Robert and his team had it running without a hitch.

Like jugglers in a culinary circus, we made our improvised dining operation work.

The team served breakfast and dinner at the Crow's Nest, shuffling in and out through the back door. We handled lunch at the pool bar and cobbled together a plan to supplement our dining options by using a small kitchen in the Canoe and Kayak Club, snugged along the waterfront on the bay side. We offered waterfront dining there, which turned out to be a big hit. In fact, guests loved it so much that even after everything was back to normal, they asked if we could keep the Canoe and Kayak Club open for dinner.

As much as I would have loved to accommodate their requests, it didn't make any sense logistically, but it was a pleasant reminder that even temporary solutions can lead to unexpected wins.

The kitchen transformation took about eleven months—longer than we had hoped. But the year turned out to be unusually slow. Unfortunately, that was due to an environmental challenge—an outbreak of red tide. While we saw fewer guests, it gave us a bit of breathing room to complete the project, though it was a stark reminder of how damaging such events can be to the island's marine environment and the local community.

In simple terms, a red tide occurs when conditions like warm water, abundant sunlight, and nutrient-rich waters promote the rapid growth of certain naturally occurring algae. This growth results in a harmful algal bloom.

Red tide produces toxins that can be lethal to marine life. Dead fish littered the island's shores and dealt a severe blow to the local fishing community when the noxious outbreak ravaged the fish population. My heart went out to the fishing guides whose livelihood took a big hit.

It was a tough year, but once we completed the new kitchen, we felt like an enormous weight had been lifted. The staff was thrilled because the new space had air-conditioning, a major upgrade from the sweltering heat of the old facility. It was fantastic. And finally, after all the challenges and obstacles, we were ready to rock and roll with a kitchen that was more than ready to handle whatever came next.

Not long after we celebrated hitting a home run with our newly renovated food and beverage workspace, life threw us a brushback fastball, like a wild pitcher determined to unnerve us. COVID-19 was a lethal pitch that came out of nowhere. One moment, we were rounding the bases, feeling great about our future. And the next, we were ducking out of the way, unsure of what it all meant and what would happen next.

I remember talking with Angie and her doctor in January 2020, when the first case was diagnosed in the U.S., and I'll never forget his words: "This thing will spread everywhere. Everyone will get it."

Soon, the virus was a global epidemic, and the world as we knew it changed. Our anniversary was March 17, just days after the U.S. declared the pandemic a national emergency. The very next day, we made the agonizing decision to shut down 'Tween Waters.

I can't fully express how surreal that moment was. Closing those doors felt like I was closing the door on a part of my life that had defined so much of who I was. The worst part was not knowing when we would be able to reopen. It wasn't just the inn that went dark—a shroud seemed to descend over everything.

Throughout March, national infection rates continued to climb. Some of our guests didn't want to return home to areas where the virus was more widespread than in Florida at that time, so we let a few stay on the property.

We shifted our focus to offering to-go meals in the food and beverage department—one of the few ways we could keep a sense of normalcy while time seemed to stand still. No one knew how long the situation would last or what the ultimate impact would be. It was a period of guessing, holding our collective breath, and hoping.

We cautiously reopened on May 1. As May turned into June, something unexpected happened: people from states where there were more restrictive lockdowns arrived in droves. It was the start of what some called "COVID revenge travel," where people, tired of restrictions, sought solace in places like ours. The summer was busier than we could have predicted, and the momentum carried well into the fall.

Even though we were picking up steam, caution still reigned when it came to our annual lighting ceremony at Thanksgiving. We skipped the traditional buffet, limiting the event to resort guests only. And while we set off fireworks, the celebration was more subdued than in years past. It wasn't the grand spectacle we were used to, but it felt important to show that we were still standing, still bringing people joy, and most importantly, that we were coming back.

Nineteen

Eyes on the Future

Reopening 'Tween Waters in the COVID era was both a relief and a cautious leap of faith—a time of uncertainty that propelled us to think more deeply about how to evolve and adapt the business.

A big step in that evolution began with implementing our succession plan. We promoted Doug Babcock to president and CEO, and I moved into the role of board chair. I'll be honest, the transition wasn't easy for me.

For decades, I'd been involved in the day-to-day operations, and I had a hands-on approach that became second nature. I enjoyed it, and I couldn't let it go overnight; I found it hard to step away from being on the operation's front lines. Doug took it all in stride and was gracious as I adjusted to my new role.

Beyond the company's leadership structure, we were transforming our business itself. We had recently brought the West

Wind Inn into the fold, and it made sense to fine-tune our corporate identity as well. We rebranded from Rochester Resorts to Sanibel Captiva Beach Resorts (SCBR) because we felt it more accurately reflected our business.

Adding the West Wind to our portfolio secured our position as the largest single entity of owned accommodations on the islands. It was a huge milestone—one that not only expanded our footprint but also brought incredible new talent into our organization with the addition of the establishment's longstanding general manager, René Affourtit.

At the time we purchased the Sanibel property, René had been its GM for twenty-five years. But that was actually his second career. His first was in the military, where he was a member of the U.S. Army's legendary Green Berets and served two tours of duty in Vietnam. As if that weren't enough, he rose through the ranks to serve as chief of staff to Secretary of Defense Caspar Weinberger in the Reagan Administration.

Believe me, you could fill an entire book with stories from his time in the military, but for now, let's just say his life's journey has been nothing short of impressive. After we finalized the deal for the West Wind, I offered René the position of chief financial officer at SCBR. A thoughtful team player, he initially said he would stick around for a couple of years to help with the transition—but here we are, a decade later, and we're still fortunate to have him on our team.

He and I don't always agree, but our discussions are thoughtful and often lead to greater understanding. He has become a mentor to many of us. Holly, our controller who has been with me for forty-five years, was apprehensive at first, but now they have breakfast together every Friday. René has also played a key role in mentoring Ola, who has grown into an exceptional director of finance.

Beyond our professional bond, René has become a dear friend to Angie and me and was a great help putting my house back together after Hurricane Ian. He and I seem to share a similar philosophy in that he will keep working as long as he feels he brings value to the company.

With 'Tween Waters, Beachview Cottages, Castaways Cottages, and the West Wind Inn under our belt, we had north of 300 units in our portfolio—a far cry from where we'd started back in 1976, when 'Tween Waters previous owners had the resort on the chopping block.

Having hit a home run with his vision for the West Wind, Doug sensed a new opportunity that would take us even further. The idea involved property management for home and condominium owners who wanted to rent out their island residences. We had abundant experience in superior guest services and facilities management, so the question Doug raised was: In what other ways could we leverage that expertise?

With so many beautiful homes and condominiums as possible rentals, we wondered if a market need was not being met. So we dipped our toe into the rental management waters and launched Sanibel Captiva Island Vacation Rentals—SCIVR for short.

We started small because we wanted to test market demand gradually and get a hands-on feel for the potential. As time passed, business was steady. Encouraged, we expanded our effort. This entailed striking a deal with Art Corace of ReMax of the Islands. Art and his son, Dustyn, were in the rental management business but decided that it didn't make economic sense for them to continue; successfully managing rental properties became far more labor-intensive than they had bargained for.

Hmm. Who knew the business could be so laborious? (*Wink, wink.*) It requires much more than listing properties and finding tenants.

The day-to-day operations are complex. First, there's ongoing property maintenance—everything from routine repairs and upkeep to unexpected emergencies like a broken AC unit or a leaky roof, which can happen at any hour of the day—or on any given holiday. It's a 24/7 proposition.

And you don't keep properties shipshape by simply fixing what breaks; you must proactively manage wear and tear so guests feel like they're staying in a well-maintained, welcoming home away from home.

Then there's guest management, a full-time job all on its own. Guests come with high expectations, especially in premier vacation destinations like Sanibel and Captiva. They expect seamless check-ins, prompt responses to issues, and a smooth checkout process. Not to mention the constant turnover of short-term rentals, which means cleaning and preparing the property for each new arrival on a tight schedule. It's a juggling act to manage people, properties, and time.

When you're dealing with multiple properties, the complexity only increases. Each property is its own little ecosystem, and making sure everything runs smoothly across a portfolio of vacation rentals requires careful coordination and attention to detail.

For Art and Dustyn, the rental business became more of a grind than they had expected—too much work, not enough return on their investment of time and energy. It was understandable, and it was easy to see why they were ready to step away from that aspect of their business.

So Doug and I reached an agreement with ReMax of the Islands to acquire its rental business. The move propelled SCIVR a giant step forward, from a handful of initial properties to managing over a hundred rental residences on Sanibel and Captiva.

Launching our rental management division was one of those developments that evolved into an entirely new facet of our business—growth that came from a willingness to take a shot at something new, even if it felt a bit like stepping into the unknown.

As we settled into managing our expanded operations, our prospects were looking brighter than ever. Having survived the challenges of the previous few years, especially the pandemic, it seemed that we had hit another gear.

Doug's vision for the future continued to push us toward new horizons. In the early summer of 2022, he laid out an ambitious expansion plan for the Crow's Nest, which the board of directors approved. The effort included building an upstairs addition that match the height of the Wakefield Room and provided sweeping views of the Gulf of Mexico.

We transformed the former Crow's Nest into the new Shipyard restaurant, while the Crow's Nest moved into the new upstairs location as a premier steakhouse—and the only second-level dining destination on the islands with a glorious beachfront view of the Gulf and its mesmerizing sunsets. It was such an exciting new chapter for our food and beverage team.

But our plans didn't stop there. As we approached this fresh burst of construction, we considered other facilities and realized we had the resources to make upgrades. With the business firing on all cylinders and revenues hitting new highs each month during the summer, we devised a plan to revamp the aging Sea Grape and Palmetto Buildings.

Striking while the iron was hot, we thought, *What the heck? Why not take care of the tennis courts too?* We decided to elevate them to create additional parking underneath. It's remarkable what's possible when both revenue and borrowing power align.

As we embraced these new ventures, our willingness to adapt and explore new opportunities proved vital to our continued success. Little did we know, even as we celebrated milestones, a different kind of storm loomed on the horizon—one that would test us as never before.

Twenty

Hurricane Ian: Chaos and Kindness

Business boomed throughout the summer of 2022, and the tropical beach weather accompanied the fantastic potential that lay ahead. But as local weather reports started to change, a sense of unease crept in.

While we marked a period of unprecedented growth, Mother Nature reminded us of her unpredictable power. On the morning of September 26, a Category 1 hurricane named Ian bore down on the western tip of Cuba with sustained winds of eighty-five mph. Most hurricane models, including those used by the National Hurricane Center (NHC), projected Tampa as the most likely landfall.

A potential threat loomed, but it was the kind we'd seen before and had grown accustomed to tracking during hurricane season. We monitored the models and NHC's reporting, as we had always done. And though we were concerned, we weren't sounding any alarms just yet. Still, an uneasy energy replaced the laid-back vibes that typically run through the islands.

By five a.m. on September 28, Hurricane Ian had exploded into a monster Category 5 storm, with winds topping a catastrophic 160 mph. We held our collective breath; even offshore, a hurricane of that magnitude spelled coastal trouble.

Though Hurricane Ian stripped away so much, it also revealed the strength of our community, the resilience of our team, and the deep bonds that held us together as we began the monumental task of rebuilding.

As it crept north, up the coast—past Marco Island, Naples, Bonita Springs—it hooked to the right like a wicked baseball slider when it was about thirty miles out. And in a flash, the threat that for days had been projected to skirt Sanibel and Captiva as it passed was churning straight at us, and the islands did their best to brace for an impact no amount of preparation could prevent.

We knew the wind would be brutal, but Ian's storm surge truly had us shaking in our boat shoes. Sanibel and Captiva, as beautiful as they are, are low-lying barrier islands, and there's little buffer between us and the Gulf when the waters begin to rise and push onshore.

Things turned chaotic after Ian set sights on us. Where would Angie and I go? What about the staff? Some of our employees had no safe place to go, so we made sure they could shelter in the Areca Building.

I tried to convince myself that 'Tween Waters would escape the worst of the storm, and I felt a cautious optimism that the resort would be safe. But beyond Ian's immediate impact, I was concerned about how long we would be without power, water, and the basic necessities once it passed. That was anyone's guess; the area had never faced a hurricane of such force and size before.

Angie and I sought refuge in our elevated Sanibel home and braced for impact, just as we had back in 2004 when Hurricane Charley tore through. Charley had also been a powerful Category 4 storm, with a wind field that only extended about eighty-five miles from the center. And it moved fast, roughly twenty-five mph, so the storm surge intensity hadn't been an issue.

Ian turned out to be a different beast. With a wind field spanning about 240 miles, the massive hurricane lumbered at nine mph as it pushed the Gulf of Mexico at Southwest Florida's coastal communities. The hurricane made landfall on Cayo Costa, a barrier island four miles north of us on the afternoon of September 28 as a massive Category 4 hurricane, with 150 mph sustained winds.

Our beachfront home faces the Gulf of Mexico, with the main living floor about fifteen feet above mean high tide. As Ian approached, ominous charcoal skies churned with stacked storm clouds, and increasing winds tugged at the trees.

Far off, over the Gulf's horizon, a deep rumble of thunder echoed—not the sharp crack of summer storms with which we were so familiar, but a slow, reverberating growl.

As the wind strengthened, it carried the Gulf's salty scent with it, and the once-calm surface rose into frothy peaked waves that crashed onshore in relentless succession.

At first, the water creeping toward us wasn't too bad, and we held a sliver of hope that maybe the angle of the incoming wind and water would work in our favor. But then a frightening thought shot through my mind: Earlier that morning, reports had trickled in about a fifty-two-foot-high wave Ian had spawned in the Gulf, seventy miles offshore.

There's no way a fifty-foot rogue wave would hit our house, I thought. And I was right. It was a seventeen- to twenty-foot high wall of water that smashed into the Gulf-side elevation of our home like a massive sledgehammer.

All hell broke loose when our panoramic Gulf-view windows shattered in an explosion of water that avalanched inside with a furious roar, churning through the room in a wind-driven maelstrom. The floor became a liquid torrent as the storm surge dragged furniture and tables around the room like dollhouse pieces. The wind screamed through the gaping breach, howling with the force of a freight train. The house, once our sanctuary, now felt like a sinking ship.

Behind the house, the tsunami-like water blew out the back wall of our garage and swept our cars away. Angie's jackknifed against some pilings, while mine careened down the driveway on the powerful surge as it spun off into the howling daggers of rain and out of sight.

Dazed and drenched, Angie and I made a frantic dash to our Japanese-inspired teahouse, a small refuge partially protected by the main house. We huddled there in pitch-black darkness, powerless, while Category 4 winds—roaring at over 140 mph—lashed the walls. Gusts flirted with 160 mph, Category 5 strength, and battered the structure relentlessly.

Every second felt like an eternity as we endured the most terrifying night of our lives. For six hours, we holed up in the darkened teahouse—ironically intended in the Japanese culture as a calming space to relax and enjoy tea with company.

When morning finally dawned, we emerged to a scene of utter destruction; what had once been a comforting, serene landscape looked like a battlefield.

The bruised sky, still thick with lingering clouds, created an eerie, muted light. Damp air smelled of saltwater and waterlogged wood. Downed trees lay scattered like fallen giants, and remnants of the destruction were everywhere. The wind still blew at around thirty mph, with higher gusts, as if Ian hadn't quite let go of its grip.

Our neighbors, Richard and Jane, slogged through the muck to check on us. Their college-age daughters trudged through mud and the debris field to pick up whatever pieces they could, while Richard and I hunted for my car. We finally found it about 200 yards away, half-submerged in a swamp. Lo and behold, a full case of bottled water had somehow found its way from Richard's garage and sat perched on the roof. You can't make this stuff up.

Back at our battered houses later that morning, just when we thought things couldn't get any worse, they did. We smelled smoke.

Three houses down the beach from ours, and only two away from Richard and Jane's, a multimillion-dollar Gulf-front home had erupted in flames—and the wind was blowing our way. Not a good sign.

Before we knew it, the inferno had jumped to the house next to Richard and Jane's—their home was next in the line of fire. There was nothing we could do but hope for the best and head for the beach to trek toward some sort of civilization.

As it turned out, because their house was constructed of materials that starved the fire of its fuel—stucco-coated concrete block and a metal roof—the structure stopped the flames from advancing any farther. The intense heat, however, blew out their windows.

As we left the fire behind and made our way along the shoreline, a team of first responders found us. They told us the Sanibel Causeway had collapsed; no vehicles could access the islands, where the roads were strewn with downed trees and other structural debris the hurricane had tossed around like pick-up sticks and Lego pieces.

We flew to an island shelter in a twin-rotor Chinook chopper, the kind of heavy-lift transport you see used in military operations. Flying over the devastation, I saw island spots I knew so well, now submerged amid a tangle of trees and debris. The islands had been hit before, but never like this.

A physical and emotional whirlwind marked the following days. Displaced, uncertain, and surrounded by the storm's wreckage, I received an unexpected call from Wandales, who worked for me in our landscaping department. Somehow, despite the spotty cell service, he got through and volunteered to pick us up at a hurricane shelter in East Fort Myers. We could then stay at his house out that way, in Lehigh Acres.

While I was immensely grateful for his generous offer, there were several stumbling blocks. One was that his house, like roughly a million others in Southwest Florida, was without power or potable water. Two, I didn't want him driving on the roads with no traffic lights, which Ian had wiped out. Finally, I needed to remain close to our home and the company's properties to help lead recovery efforts. So, although I appreciated Wandales' kindness, I had to decline.

That meant Angie and I slept on the hallway floor of a local school that served as a shelter. It was a long night. No air-conditioning to fight the damp heat, no reliable communication with the outside world, and a single malfunctioning bathroom shared by 200 people.

The next day, our food and beverage director, Laurent Bosc, came to our rescue. Laurent had been with us through thick and thin, and his offer of hospitality was a much-needed reprieve. He picked us up and took us to his livable house in Fort Myers, where we stayed for three nights.

Angie and I had left our house with only the clothes on our backs, so an impromptu "shopping spree" at Publix's souvenir apparel racks became our source for some makeshift clothing. It was an odd stretch of time: one minute, we slept on a shelter floor, and the next we wandered the aisles of a barely functioning grocery store as we tried to claw back some sense of normalcy.

While we were with Laurent, our neighbors Richard and Jane generously arranged a fishing guide so we could check on the condition of our house and retrieve Angie's prescription medicines, which we had left behind in the chaos after Ian.

During this time, police patrolled the waters and had locked down movement on the islands. Once we were out on the water, they stopped us and reminded us of the strict emergency protocols regarding movement around the islands.

But Angie explained how important it was that she retrieve her medications. Luckily for us, they understood how all our lives had been turned upside down and let us pass.

Once restrictions were relaxed a few days later, Angie and I arranged a second trip to the house to salvage whatever we could with fishing guide Colin Carpenter, who worked out of the 'Tween Waters marina. He picked us up early in the morning. The Gulf was calm; after the raging waters Ian had whipped up, that was a welcomed sight. As the boat's white wake fanned out behind us, the salty air in my face helped to clear my thoughts, and I felt a rush of determination over what lay ahead.

The ravaged bleakness of our home broke our hearts. We took a couple of hours to sift through what was left. Colin was an absolute godsend, helping me pull out cherished items like our Oriental rugs, which had been destroyed. Every item we saved carried weight—not in material value, but in the memories they held.

But as we went through our home, Angie made a heartrending discovery: looters had already picked through the personal treasures we'd collected during our fifty years together. The pain of seeing our life's mementos stolen was less about their value and more about the emotional scars it left.

Even in the face of that loss, however, we focused on recovering what we could. When I asked Colin what I owed him for his help, he gave me a weary but warm smile and said, "Tony, 'Tween Waters has meant so much to me, so a couple of beers will do when things are up and running again."

His gesture was immensely kind, especially since his own house had suffered damage and he had his own life to reclaim. Ian hit the fishing guides hard, with their work reduced to ferrying people around the islands and back and forth to the mainland. While his offer touched me, I insisted on paying him accordingly for his time and effort.

A few days later, I was able to get in touch with my longtime friend Joe Mazzola, who had a two-bedroom, two-bath villa with power, and he invited us to stay with him. It was a blessing beyond measure. It turned out he was heading up to Georgia for six to eight weeks and said we could stay as long as we needed; he even gave us full use of his car! What a remarkable friend. Otherwise, we would have been homeless.

As the weeks wore on, Publix became everyone's hero, keeping goods stocked the best they could. It would be a nearly a month before the general public could drive across the causeway, which Ian had demolished and rendered impassible; prior to that, emergency vehicles and some utility crews were allowed limited access to help with recovery efforts and restore essential services. Such destruction to this vital transportation infrastructure set us back more than sixty years, to the days before 1963 when Sanibel and Captiva were accessible only by ferry.

Some said it would take six months to a year to restore the bridge. But Governor Ron DeSantis cut through the red tape and kicked repairs into high gear, launching a massive plan to implement a temporary fix and reconnect us to the mainland, which was vital for recovery efforts.

The storm surge had washed away sections of the causeway on the two island strips that support the water-level sections. Equally disastrous, Ian wrecked three of the bridge's ramps that serve as transitions from water level to the elevated roadway spans.

Under the governor's orders, the Florida Department of Transportation mobilized contractors to begin emergency repairs. Crews worked around the clock, often relying on boats and barges to transport heavy equipment and materials.

Despite the logistical challenges and the scale of the damage, crews completed the temporary repairs faster than anyone thought possible; the causeway reopened within fifteen days after the project started. These repairs allowed critical access for restoration work on the island until the permanent causeway reconstruction could begin. We were so appreciative of Governor DeSantis' efforts and his "get to work and fix it" approach.

On the fateful day Hurricane Ian unleashed his fury, we confronted a challenge unlike any before, both in our personal and professional lives. The devastation was staggering. But even amid the chaos and destruction, the islands, along with all of Southwest Florida, found strength in each other and a renewed determination to bounce back in the face of enormous loss.

Twenty-One

From Destruction to Determination

As the passing days and weeks after Hurricane Ian turned into months, we grasped the magnitude of what had been lost. The storm ravaged homes, businesses, and lives, and the road to recovery looked impossibly daunting. Yet, amid the wreckage, there was a community spirit of resilience and unity that would guide us through the difficult times ahead.

Before construction crews restored access to the islands, Doug contracted with a restoration company to rent out 'Tween Waters in order to support not just our own rebuilding efforts but also those of other islanders.

The inn became a dynamic hub of activity, with teams working relentlessly to restore the area. In the meantime, our incredible employees stepped up in ways I'll never forget. In Ian's aftermath, the causeway was closed to the general public for almost a month, so our staff used boats to ferry essential supplies—food, water, whatever was needed—to those who had stayed on the islands, braving the difficult conditions. Everyone pitched in without hesitation to help where they could.

Our chef, John Feagans, was also essential in getting things back on track. He and his team opened the kitchen at 'Tween Waters under grueling circumstances and kept it running for two months, feeding upward of a hundred workers each day. That kind of effort made all the difference in keeping the recovery going at full speed.

The Captiva Island Fire Control District played a pivotal role as well, and we worked hand in glove with them. As a first responder, Fire Chief Jeff Pawul worked tirelessly to help the island get back on its feet. That kind of dedication kept everything moving forward when it felt like so much was standing in our way.

After about two months, Doug ended the contract with the restoration company staying at 'Tween Waters, and we were ready to reopen to the public. Our first guests were primarily anxious island property owners who needed a place to stay while they checked on the status of their homes, along with the construction workers they had hired to rebuild.

Once again, we tackled our "he who opens first wins" credo head-on. Of course, the work wasn't done. Repairs were still ongoing, and we had to continue finishing the Shipyard restaurant in what had been the Crow's Nest space. But with the builder still under contract from before the hurricane, we pushed forward with confidence the hard work would pay off.

We also set the wheels in motion for our other major projects: renovating the Sea Grape and Palmetto buildings and raising the tennis courts to improve parking. We were committed to rebounding, and the sense of progress was undeniable.

In the aftermath of Ian, we decided to replace the roofs atop every building on the property. With the storm damage still fresh, it felt like the right move to ensure that everything was up to the new standard we were setting for the future of 'Tween Waters and our other properties.

However, the recovery was far from smooth. We had no internet for quite some time, which made coordination and communication even more challenging than usual. But one of the biggest hurdles we encountered was getting people and materials to the island.

The bridge traffic was a nightmare. For months, a torrent of restoration company vehicles, trades workers, and other contractors clogged the three-mile causeway as they converged on the island. The gridlock left people backed up for an hour and a half, sometimes two, just to reach the toll booth at Punta Rassa.

The bottleneck not only slowed everything down, but it made life especially difficult for our employees who had to commute daily to and from the island. To ease their burden, we tried to compensate them in small ways, like giving them Publix gift cards to help cover what they needed.

As we assessed the full extent of our damages, we needed a solid plan to guide us into the future. For 'Tween Waters, that plan was simple: fix it up to a new standard of quality.

But Beach View Cottages? That was a different story. Those twenty-two units were demolished. New building codes required us to elevate the property to seventeen feet, which would fundamentally change the cherished look and feel of the original cottages.

It was a tough pill to swallow, but we're pushing forward with a new design, and we plan to break ground in late 2024. We expect the cost to be around $13 million, and our goal is to reopen in late 2025 or early 2026.

Then there was West Wind, and that presented a real puzzle. We could spend $10 million to $12 million to restore the existing structure, but we'd be left with small rooms and ground-floor units that could flood again. The other option was to knock it down and start fresh.

Given that it's the largest hotel on the islands—with 104 units, a restaurant, and a commercial laundry—we knew rebuilding from the ground up would be an enormous investment. But we also realized we had to make it happen. We targeted breaking ground in late 2025 or early 2026, with a two-year build-out costing around $70 million. It's a staggering number, but we have to do it to top-quality standards.

Castaways was another major loss. Thirty-eight units were wiped clean off the map, but not from our memories. We plan to look at that project in 2025. But for now, the focus is on rebuilding what's possible within time constraints.

One thing Doug and I decided early on was to hire a demolition company to clear the debris from our severely damaged properties and get it to the curb, where FEMA could pick it up. It was a smart move. I'm certain it saved us close to a million dollars, if not more. Some folks didn't take advantage of that, and it ended up costing them in the long run.

As for SCIVR, we lost a substantial number of managed properties, but we kept a small group of core employees to keep the business afloat. We're slowly bringing those properties back into the fold, but it will be another two years before SCIVR is fully operational again.

Though Hurricane Ian stripped away so much, it also revealed the strength of our community, the resilience of our team, and the deep bonds that hold us together. As we began the monumental task of rebuilding, we held on to the lessons we had learned and the friendships that had carried us through the darkest of times.

The journey was far from over, but we were ready to face whatever came next, determined to rebuild stronger and smarter. Similarly, island residents and businesses strove to bounce back with resilience and determination.

Amid the chaos Ian fueled, the kindness shown to Angie and me when we needed it most meant more than words can express. It's moments like those that remind you of what really matters when everything else is washed away.

With a plan in place for the next two to three years, we're on a forward path. But as we've learned, especially after a life-altering event like Ian, the future can be full of surprises.

Twenty-Two

The Changing Tides of Work

During the preceding fifty years or so as an island innkeeper, I've learned to expect the unexpected. As we have moved through 2024 and look ahead at 2025 and beyond, I can see that the future of Beachview Cottages and the West Wind Island Resort is going to be markedly different. We have solid plans in place to reconstruct them, but their structures and appearances will change significantly—consequently, they will come with a necessary higher price point because of a converging range of rising costs.

In addition to the construction dollars to rebuild to existing codes, another huge challenge is skyrocketing property insurance rates. The firm CBRE, a commercial real estate services and investment company, reports that over the past few years, premiums for coastal properties such as those on Sanibel and Captiva have risen sharply—some have increased by twenty-five percent to as much as 150 percent. These jumps are because of the recent rise in more frequent and severe storms, which have led to an increase in insured losses.

General liability coverage also has gone through the roof. Why? Well, a big reason is because so many people are eager to file lawsuits, even when they are the knuckleheads whose foolish decisions caused the issues they are suing over! So businesses are forced to take on the greater financial burden of increased protection from lawsuits.

Beyond property and liability protection, health insurance costs have also ballooned, which hits both the company and our employees hard.

Premiums have climbed year after year. In fact, according to a study by the Kaiser Family Foundation, as of 2024 the average premium for employer-sponsored family coverage has jumped fifteen percent in just the last two years. For 2025, the trend shows no signs of slowing down.

As rising costs compel us to adapt in so many ways, there is a parallel, interconnected matter, and it has to do with balancing employee expectations with business realities. In a nutshell, the financial pressures we face are only half the equation; the other half is ensuring we have a team that's motivated and engaged.

So, I'd like to share my thoughts on the issue of work-life balance. Let me start by saying that balancing personal needs with the demands of employment isn't always easy—and that includes for me.

I think it's important to be clear-eyed about the fact that there's a natural pressure point between the fundamentals of doing business and the desire for employees to have space for their lives outside of work. I understand there's a need for family time, personal pursuits, and so forth. And I've always believed that happy, fulfilled folks make the best team members. That's the culture we've always strived to create.

For some context and perspective, my work experience has been different; the notion of work-life balance simply wasn't part of my reality as I came of age.

Working my way up, I put my head down and worked until the job was done. With 'Tween Waters, I was fully invested in building the business. That's just the way I was wired, dating back to my nose-to-the-grindstone perseverance when it came to my boyhood projects around my parents' Rochester house. In all honesty, it was that very work ethic that led to my opportunity with Lloyd and 'Tween Waters.

Let me say right up front that I also recognize I didn't have children to raise, so there wasn't that pull to carve out more personal time. The bottom line is, I didn't face the same issues prevalent today, when work-life balance is key. I understand and respect that.

But there's another side to the coin that I think tends to be overlooked in the conversation, especially when you're running a business that generates the jobs that support families with wages and benefits, along with tax dollars that help sustain communities—not only tax dollars generated by our company but also by businesses throughout the area whose shops, restaurants, and services our guests patronize and help keep afloat.

This is where the clear-eyed reality I mentioned comes into play. Sanibel Captiva Beach Resorts, like any company, operates in a competitive world where costs are climbing. Balancing staff members' personal time with the need to compete and succeed is a challenge, especially when deadlines loom or when the unexpected happens—because, trust me, in this business, the unexpected happens all the time.

The challenge is finding that middle ground—being understanding of personal needs while keeping the lights on and the doors open. A balance where staff feel supported in their personal lives, but also understand that sometimes their livelihood will ask for that extra bit of commitment. Establishing that mutual medium is tough, and I'm not going to pretend I have all the answers, but it's something I continue to strive for.

Beyond the impact of work-life balance, when it comes to the changing business landscape, wages loom large. I don't think anyone would argue against paying people a fair wage. Earning power needs to keep pace with the cost of living, but continually rising wages combined with all the other escalating expenses puts a vise on an already tight budget.

The preceding factors have reshaped what it means to do business, and their impact will drive an increase in room rates for our planned Beachview Cottages and the West Wind. There's no way around it. To cover our increased costs and provide the level of service our guests expect, we have to adjust pricing. Raising rates is not something we take lightly, but the local hospitality landscape has transformed dramatically over the past five years, and we've had to evolve with it.

As valuable as it is to accommodate different work ethics, I can't help but feel there's an essential element missing—something that ultimately boils down to personal commitment. This might sound old-fashioned, but to me, it's simply common sense.

When I landed my first job as a mason's helper in the late 1960s, I had the good fortune of working alongside Rick Pakusch, a highly skilled German mason. I learned the trade from him as we built a boathouse at my parents' Rochester home.

I clearly understood that work started at seven a.m. By 7:05, I was throwing sand and mortar into the mixer with a clear plan for the day. I wasn't wandering around in my concrete-caked boots, wondering what to do next.

One of the most valuable lessons I took from that experience was that a skilled worker should always be a step or two ahead and anticipate the next phase of a project, even before he's called upon.

What frustrates me most about the approach to work I too often see today is the amount of wasted time, usually because of poor planning and a lack of commitment to staying organized.

If I were a painter and arrived on the job at seven a.m., I would be painting by 7:05, not drifting around trying to figure out what I'm going to do for the day—I would plan ahead and know at the end of the previous day what I needed to get done the following day.

Call it preparedness, organization, self-discipline, or whatever you'd like, but to me, it's the backbone of being productive, and it respects everyone's time. Just as work-life balance aims to protect personal hours, thoughtful organization on the job can elevate the quality of everyone's work life.

As much as I value workplace efficiency, there's something to be said for how technology—particularly cell phones—has changed the way we communicate. Sometimes for the better. Sometimes not. Like any tool, they can be used well or poorly.

Texts allow for quick messages and updates, which can be beneficial. But texting has its limitations, the same as email.

My biggest concern is when an issue arises and I see emails or texts flying back and forth; it's like a detached flailing around to find an answer. The problem is texts and emails can be misunderstood; for all their convenience, such instant communication (emojis or not) can easily give the wrong impression.

There's a reason I prefer to tackle important matters face-to-face. Bringing everyone into the same room is advantageous because you cut through confusion instantly and can address issues head-on, in real time. To me, that's the gold standard of communication, especially when leaders are involved in the conversation.

A related issue is that it's so easy for people today to operate in silos, to focus only on their specific role without seeing the bigger picture, as if they exist in a vacuum. It's frustrating to see people working only within their narrow scope and saying, "It's not my job."

There was a time when I would hire someone and hand them a blank sheet of paper, chuckle, and tell them, "This is a list of things you don't have to do." I'm sure HR would have a field day with that today.

While being planful is essential to success, it's clear to me that planning is only part of the picture. There's also the *commitment* behind every plan. There's a saying that's been around forever because it's on target, and it bears repeating: "Under promise and over deliver." Nothing feels worse to me than making a promise on which I fail to deliver. Or I forget to deliver amid the hectic pace of the everyday.

A memory comes to mind whenever I think about personal commitment and follow-through. Years ago, I reconnected with a former classmate from my high school days at Manlius Military Academy in Upstate New York.

His name is Gary Steele, who went on to graduate from the United States Military Academy at West Point and made West Point history as the first African-American football player to earn a varsity letter, breaking significant racial barriers in collegiate sports during the 1960s. But he was more than just a great athlete. He's always been a great individual.

The chance for us to catch up with each other over a shared, formative experience came when Manlius honored Gary for his lifetime achievements, including his twenty-three-year career in the Army. (Manlius merged in 1970 with Pebble Hill School and is now known as Manlius Pebble Hill.) Floyd Little, the legendary Syracuse football player and NFL Hall of Famer, presented Gary's award and gave a powerful speech.

After the ceremony, Gary and I grabbed a cup of coffee and caught up on the course of our lives since parting ways in 1965. He shared something that has stuck with me ever since: the West Point Cadet Prayer.

One line of that prayer has been my anchor ever since, something I've kept in my journal to reflect on daily. It says, *"Make us to choose the harder right instead of the easier wrong, and never to be content with a half-truth when the whole can be won."*

Those words capture an honesty and a commitment I think are worth striving for. To me, commitment is what underlies performance and the way we choose to live our lives, empowering us to face each day with purpose, even when challenges arise.

But commitment alone isn't enough—its true value is only revealed when we're tested. Measuring performance is easy when the waters are calm—everyone is a star when there's no pressure. But *real* performance? That emerges in the storm, when routines dissolve and easy paths disappear. "When the going gets tough, the tough get going" may be a cliché, but that's the attitude that will win the day.

Picture a busy restaurant where, on an average night, every server seems equally assured. But when the rush hits, tables fill, orders pile up, and the pace races, a divide emerges. The best servers get sharper, quicker, more focused, and make fewer mistakes despite the clamor and chaos. Others, overwhelmed, get lost in the weeds and panic sets in.

Leadership follows the same principle. I've learned that the real measure of leadership is how one reacts under pressure. That's when you see who steps up and truly leads. When all is well, practically anyone in a leadership position can move assuredly through the routines of the job. But true leadership emerges during troublesome times. Great leaders don't shrink. They *think*. And they calmly anchor their teams, create positive momentum toward answers, and face challenges head-on.

Others, when faced with the same adversity, react differently. Some fold. Instead of guiding their teams, they get mired in frustration or a "why is this happening to me" defeatist mentality.

True leadership under pressure, though, isn't about, "Why me?" It's about, "What's next? And how do I figure things out and move forward to a thoughtful solution?"

Twenty-Three

Navigating What's Next

THINKING ABOUT WHAT IT means to lead through times of adversity brings me to the inevitable question of, "What comes next?"

As I consider the future, I often ask myself, "How much longer do I want to keep coming to work?" My answer is straightforward: as long as I can bring value. If I can contribute through the wisdom I've gathered, the knowledge of what's worked (and what hasn't), and my insights from decades of experience, then it's worthwhile. But if I ever feel as if I'm just taking up space, that will be my cue to step aside.

Beyond my role in the company, I also find real joy in supporting the island community. My involvement with the Captiva Island Historical Society has been deeply rewarding; each meeting with the board of directors brings fresh perspectives and a sense of connection to the island's rich past. Serving on the United

Way board for over twenty-five years has been similarly fulfilling. It's given me a window into the needs of our community, on the island and beyond, deepening my understanding of the challenges our neighbors face.

Team members with 20+ years of dedication. (Left to right) Front row: René, Holly, Yours Truly, Dan, Cindy. Middle row: Marissa, Rene, Lauriston, Alex, Ariel, Jacquelin. Back row: Oleksandr, Samuel, Ola, Ludget.

The Captiva Community Panel (CCP) has also been a valuable connection point. Because Captiva is part of unincorporated Lee County, the CCP is our primary voice in local matters. As an advisory board to the Lee County Board of Commissioners, the organization keeps me grounded in the issues affecting our area.

My time on the board of the Charitable Foundation of the Islands (CFI) has been a particular highlight as well. In fact, my work there involved one of the best boards on which I've had the privilege to serve.

As life continues to unfold, I can't help but think about how much I've enjoyed being a steward of historic 'Tween Waters. When the time comes to step away, I know I'll miss the relationships I've had over these many years with guests, employees, and our vendors.

Memories are funny things... over time, they can become like old photographs left out in the sun. The edges may blur a bit, colors soften, and the once-sharp details can settle into a gentle impression. All I know is that recounting these stories has been a complete joy.

I know I've left out some tales, guests, and employees—perhaps too numerous to count. But I wanted to share what I could with all of you. If you have any questions, please feel free to email me. Maybe even mail me a note. (People still occasionally do that, right?)

Okay, folks, I'm no Randy Wayne White, the prodigious local author; this book of tales is a "one and done." And as I wrapped things up, Hurricane Helene was on our radar. Thankfully, she blew through with relatively minimal effects, and our thoughts went out to our northern neighbors in the Big Bend area and those in the Southeast so heavily impacted, particularly North Carolina.

With Helene past, it wasn't long before Milton was churning our way in the Gulf. So I said a quick prayer, only half in jest, that went something like this: "Lord, I've turned my cheek once, and then twice. If I need to go with another cheek, it's gonna be below my waist."

In a bit of déjà vu, Milton's approach reminded me of Thanksgiving 2022, when I'd planned a family reunion for about twenty-four of us, only to have it canceled by Hurricane Ian. Two years later, I had reignited those plans, but then we were in the same situation, with a storm threatening to crash the party.

I dashed off an email to my family and quoted three songs that captured my mood: *"... this could be the last time, maybe the last time, I don't know..."* from the Rolling Stones' tune "Last Time." Then there was "Do That to Me One More Time" by Captain & Tennille. And, of course, Gloria Gaynor's "I Will Survive."

Hurricane Milton created havoc here in Southwest Florida as it spun off tornadoes, and the storm ravaged our properties' vegetation. But I'm grateful that 'Tween Waters, the historic cottages, and the restaurants remained intact, and we were ready to reopen within a week.

So I figured what the heck, and I emailed another invitation to my family with a line from Starship's 1987 hit "Nothing's Gonna Stop Us Now." I was flooded with responses from relatives eager to join in the reunion.

I'm sure Mother Nature will spin up future storms. That's just a bit of a toll we pay for living in a tropical paradise. And, surely, there will continue to be twists and turns, but I feel confident that the team we have in place will always stand tall and meet the challenges head-on.

And with that, I want to thank you all for spending some time with me and joining in on my tales of an island innkeeper. Let's see where life leads next.

Kind regards,

Tony

Special Thanks

Tony and Angie relax on their patio.

First, to my wife Angie for all her emotional and financial help during those early years. I couldn't have done it without her.

To the many friendships that have shaped my life over these past 50 years. I want to express my heartfelt gratitude to each and every one of you. Forgive me if I inadvertently forget to mention you by name, and please know that your kindness and presence have meant the world to me. Without your loyalty and support, the road would have been much tougher.

Thank you Brian and Deirde, Allen and Linda, Mike and Diane, Ken and Linda, Scott and Tracy, Mike and Tricia, Peter and Jeanne, Jeff and Kristie, Anthony and Linda, Les and Susan, Steve and Jeannie, Mike and Angie, John and Candy, Peter and Carole, Bob and Jane, Sharon and Rae, Brian and Donna, Jack and Kutzi, and Henry and Diane. Also David, Cheryl, and Annie. And I can't forget Maureen, Stu, Weezie, Susan, and Patricia.

To all the dedicated staff members, past and present, who have given me so many memorable moments and whose dedication has helped create and sustain such a special place as 'Tween Waters. And to my vendors who helped support us in good times and not so good times.

Finally, to the new friendship of Bill Schreiber, who helped me put my stories on paper.

Business Friends and Partners

OVER THE YEARS, MY journey has been enriched not just by the work I've done but by those who have shared the road with me, through good times and tough times. Some began as colleagues, others as collaborators, and many have grown into cherished friends.

Together, we've built more than friendships and partnerships—we've built community and created lasting memories for all we've had the pleasure to welcome.

I would like to recognize local businesses and organizations and express my gratitude for the camaraderie and mutual support that have made my journey truly meaningful.

The Bailey Family (The Island Store), Andreas Bieri (The Mucky Duck), Sandy Stilwell Youngquist (Captiva Island Inn, Cantina Captiva, Key Lime Bistro, Latté Da, RC Otter's Island Eats, Sunshine Seafood Café and Wine Bar), Jamie and Katie Farqhuarson (The Bubble Room), the Roberts Family (Royal Shell), the Jensen Family (Jensen's Twin Palms Marina and

Cottages), Fred Hawkins (South Seas Resort), Bob and Jenny Rando, and Brad and Leslie Junghans, (Captiva Cruises), Tim McGowan (The Green Flash), Marcel Ventura (YOLO Watersports).

Our current fishing guides at 'Tween Waters: Jimbo, Randy, Jimmy, Joey, John Houston, Colin Carpenter, Rob McKay.

Former fishing guides at 'Tween Waters: Bob Sabatino, Mike Fuery, Jerry Way, Duke Sells.

Sanibel Captiva Organizations: Captiva Civic Association, Captiva Community Panel, Captiva Island Historical Society, Captiva Chapel by the Sea, Sanibel Captiva Trust Company, Sanibel Captiva Chamber of Commerce, Charitable Foundation of the Islands.

About the Storyteller

Tony Lapi, Chairman of the Board of Sanibel Captiva Beach Resorts, has built a storied career over the course of fifty years on the islands.

He has served on many local and regional tourism boards and is a past chairman of VISIT FLORIDA, one of the most respected tourism promotion organizations in the United States. He has also served on a host of Sanibel and Captiva nonprofit organization boards.

His leadership reflects his deep belief that success isn't just about individual accomplishments but about bringing people together to achieve something greater, whether building a business, strengthening a community, or fostering personal relationships. Reflecting this commitment, he is donating all sales proceeds from the book to the Captiva Island Historical Society.

Photo Credits

Nick Adams (pages 34, 95, 118, 198); Captiva Island Historical Society (page 92)

Additional Resources

For a treasure trove of additional information about the history of 'Tween Waters Inn and Captiva Island—including archival photos, print materials, and a selection of audio recordings and documentaries—visit the Captiva Island Historical Society. http://www.captivaislandhistoricalsociety.org/

www.ingramcontent.com/pod-product-compliance
Lightning Source LLC
Chambersburg PA
CBHW062059080426
42734CB00012B/2697